BRUNO SCHULZ

New Readings, New Meanings
Nouvelles lectures, nouvelles significations

I0820626

Proceedings of the International Conference
Actes du colloque international
Montréal, Québec, Canada. May 4-5, 2007.

Organizers • Organisateurs :
Polish Institute of Arts and Sciences in Canada, Montreal
McGill University, Montreal, Canada
Polish Academy of Arts and Sciences, Cracow, Poland
Adam Mickiewicz Institute, Warsaw, Poland

Sponsors • Commanditaires :
Senate of the Republic of Poland, Warsaw, Poland
Embassy of the Republic of Poland, Ottawa, Canada
Consulate General of the Republic of Poland, Montreal, Canada
Book Institute, Cracow, Poland
La Corporation Québec-Pologne pour les Arts, Montréal, Canada

Editorial Committee • Comité de Rédaction :
Stanisław Latek
Hanna M. Pappius
Stefan Władysiuk

Proofreading • Correction
Krystyna Sokołowska

Cover & Artistic Direction • Couverture et direction de création
Alfred Hałasa

Page Layout • Mise en page
Bartosz Walczak

Tęsknota za pełnią dzieciństwa jest stara jak sztuka. Ale nikt dotychczas nie uczynił z tego dążenia naczelnego programu swej twórczości i nie ziścił go w literaturze z taką doskonałością.

La nostalgie de l'enfance est vieille comme l'art. Mais personne avant Schulz n'en fait le thème principal de son programme artistique, et ne l'a jamais exploité avec autant de perfection dans la littérature.

Longing for the fullness of childhood is as old as art itself, but Bruno Schulz turned this longing into the primary focus of his literary art.

Jerzy Ficowski

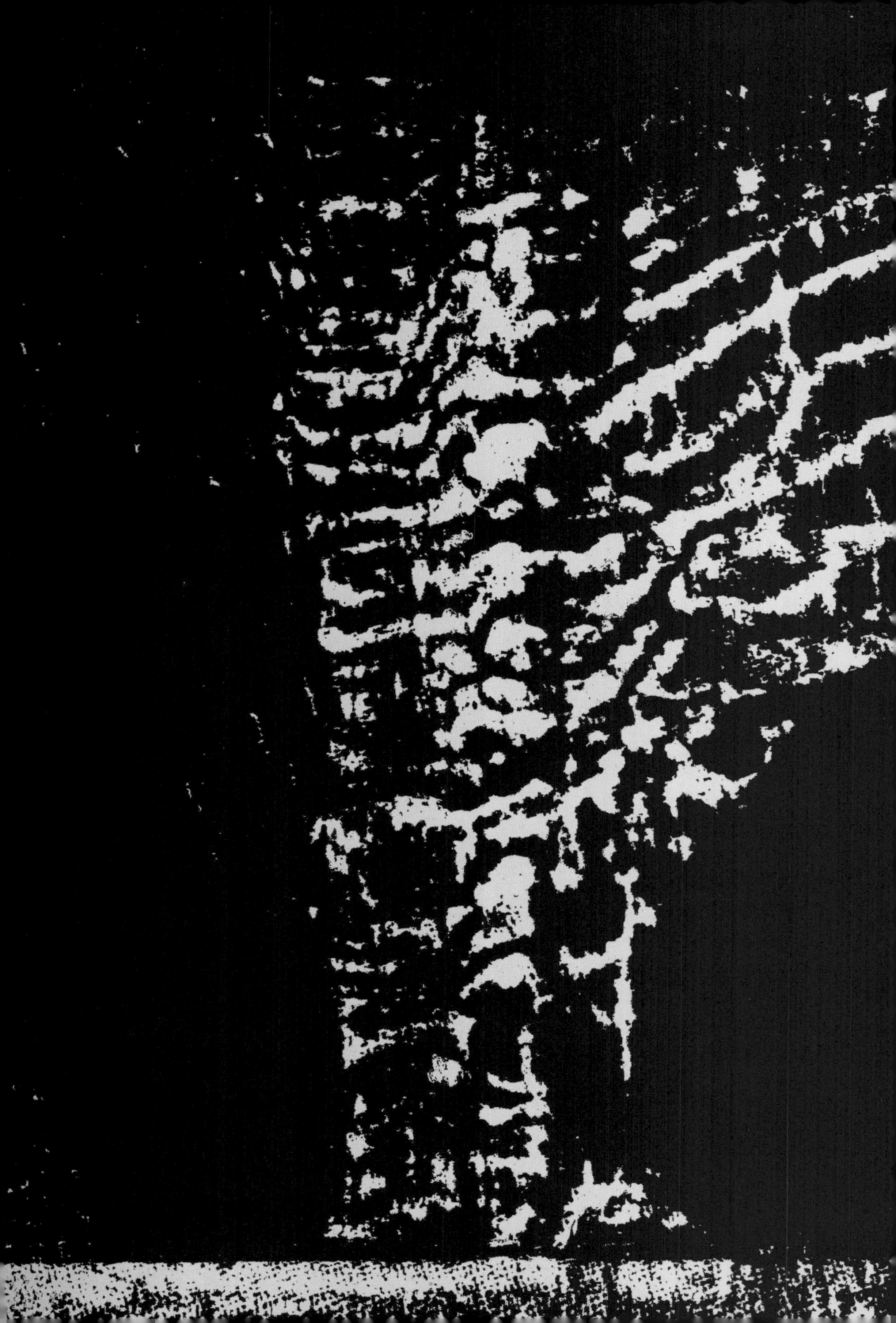

BRUNO SCHULZ

New Readings, New Meanings
Nouvelles lectures, nouvelles significations

Published under the direction of • Publié sous la direction de
Stanisław LATEK

Polish Institute of Arts and Sciences in Canada
L'Institut polonais des arts et des sciences au Canada
Montréal, Québec, Canada

Polish Academy of Arts and Sciences
L'Académie polonaise des sciences et des letters
Cracow, Poland / Cracovie, Pologne
2009

5

Copyright by:

Polish Institute of Arts and Sciences in Canada
3479 Peel Street, McGill University
Montreal, Québec, Canada
H3A 1W7
e-mail: stan.latek@mail.mcgill.ca

Polish Academy of Arts and Sciences
ul. Sławkowska 17
30-016 Kraków
Poland
e-mail: wydawnictwo@pau.krakow.pl

ISBN
978-0-9692784-8-1

ISBN
978-83-7676-018-6

Printing • Imprimé par
Poligrafia Inspektoratu Towarzystwa Salezjańskiego

Contents • Table des matières

Contents • Table des matières

List of Participants • Liste des participants

HUNDERT, Gershon, Professor, Department of Jewish Studies
McGill University, Montreal, QC, Canada

KRYSIŃSKI, Włodzimierz, Professeur, Département de littérature comparée
Université de Montréal, Montréal, QC, Canada

JARZĘBSKI, Jerzy, Professor, Department of Polish Studies
Jagiellonian University, Cracow, Poland

RAVVIN, Norman, Assistant Professor, Institute for Canadian Jewish Studies,
Concordia University, Montreal, QC, Canada

VAN HEUCKELOM, Kris, Assistant Professor, Polish Language and Literature
Katholieke Universiteit, Leuven, Belgium

GOLDFARB, David A., Assistant Professor, Slavic Department, Barnard College,
Columbia University, New York, NY, USA

SMORĄG-GOLDBERG, Małgorzata, Etudes Slaves
Université Paris IV – Sorbonne, Paris, France

MENIOK, Vira, Director, Igor Meniok Polish Studies Research Center
Ivan Franko Drohobycz State Pedagogical University, Drohobycz, Ukraine

POPRZĘCKA, Maria, Professor, Institute of Art History,
Warsaw University, Warsaw, Poland

VILLNEUVE, Johanne, Professeure, Département d'études littéraires,
Université du Quebèc à Montréal, Montréal, QC, Canada

FICOWSKA, Elżbieta, Association "Children of the Holocaust" in Poland,
President

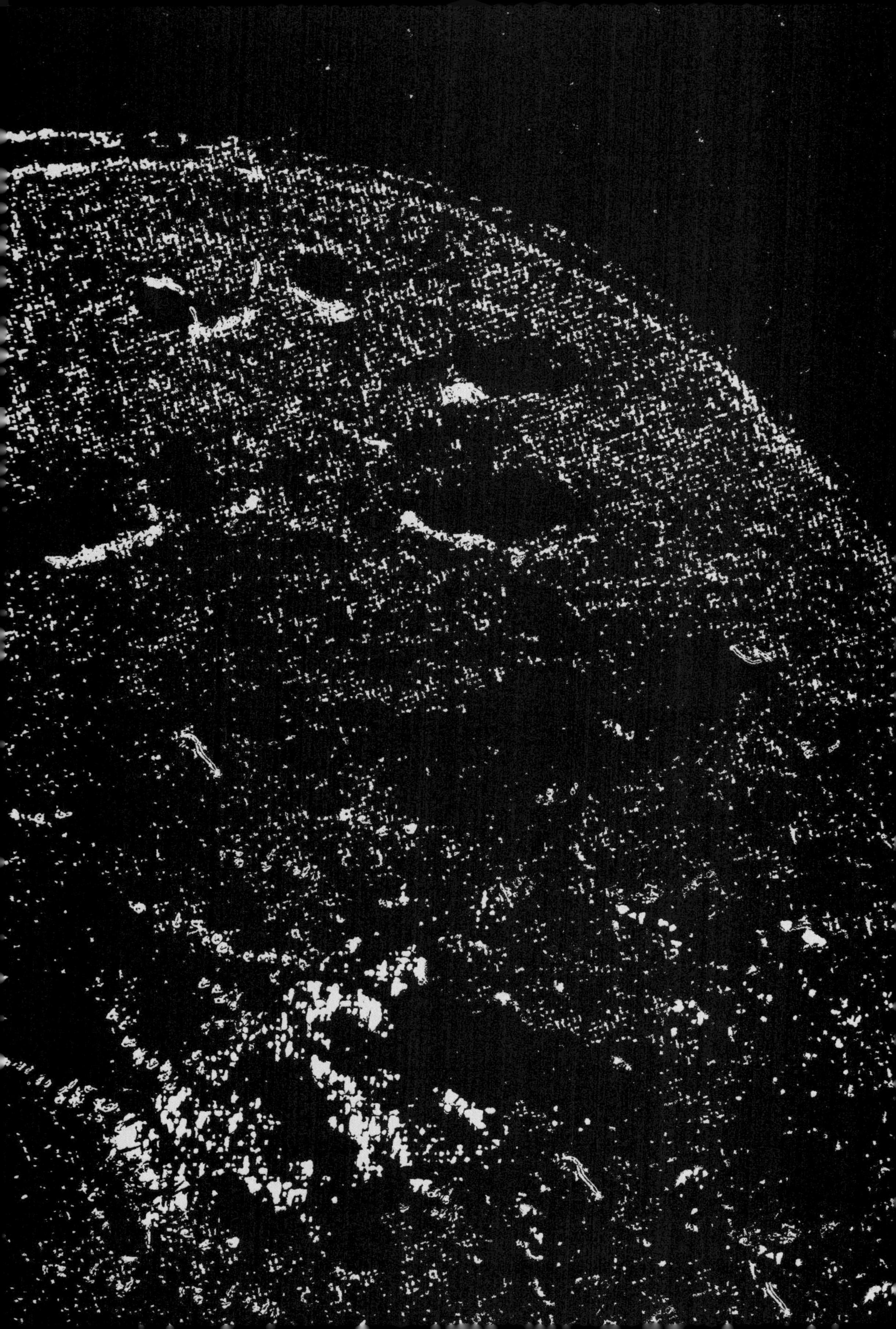

Introduction

Stanisław Latek - Polish Institute of Arts and Sciences in Canada

The present publication compiles the papers delivered during the International Bruno Schulz Symposium organized by the Polish Institute of Arts and Sciences in Canada at McGill University in Montreal on May 4th and 5th, 2007. This event brought together speakers from six countries and ten different universities.

The program of the Symposium was conceived to reflect the extraordinary complexity of Schulz's work, and to illustrate how, despite being peripheral, his work signals some of the great themes of art in the 21st century.

We, the organizers, earnestly tried to grasp the **Whole** of Schulz's work. How futile this attempt was, we realized only later, after listening to Jerzy Jarzębski's keynote lecture *Schulz: Universality and the Poetics of the Fragment* in which he stated: "(Schulz's) world is dominated by visions of the fragmentariness of reality in all its incompleteness and minuteness as well as of the fragmentariness of the text." Since so few of Schulz's works survived to our time, we may only reflect on fragments of the fragmentariness.

The collection opens with an article which barely mentions the name of Bruno Schulz. In fact, professor Gershon Hundert, one of the leading specialists of Polish and Lithuanian Jewish History investigates the puzzling question: why so many mystics and artists originated from Drohobycz, the city which serves as a backdrop for Schulz's art.

In the following article, Włodzimierz Krysiński's comparative approach confronts Schulz's prose with a variety of authors and literary styles, notably the baroque. Then, Norman Ravvin's paper offers an interesting reflection on the myth generating power of Schulz and its influence on the work of other writers. Kris Van Heuckelom for his part analyzes the idolatrous motifs in Schulz's writing, giving special attention to *Manekiny* (Tailors' Dummies) cycle from *Sklepy cynamonowe* (Cinnamon Shops), while David Goldfarb brilliantly wrestles with and guides us through the notion of "pałuby" present in the same *Manekiny* cycle, a notion he considers to be indispensable to understand Polish prewar avant-garde literature.

In her very original interpretation of one of Schulz's short stories, *Wichura* (The Gale), Małgorzata Smorąg-Goldberg examines the metaphorisation process of the writer's artistic language. Through it, she analyzes Schulz's reflection on his own Jewish condition.

Coming directly from Drochobycz, Vira Meniok took us on an extraordinary walk through Schulz's native city. Her journey starts with topographical fragments of the city and opens up on the Universe. Next, Maria Poprzęcka disputes the simplistic interpretations which have prevented a more complex and complete appreciation of Schulz's visual work.

Across from Schulz's family home, on the other side of the Drohobycz market there was a cinema owned by his brother Izydor, where Bruno hung out frequently. In her paper, Johanne Villeneuve analyzes the influence of Schulz's work on contemporary film. Her illustrated presentation was complemented by a projection of *The Street of Crocodiles*, an animated film by the Quay Brothers.

Our Symposium's special guest was Mrs. Elżbieta Ficowska, widow of the late Jerzy Ficowski, one of Poland's leading poets renowned for resurrecting Bruno Schulz's work. Jerzy Ficowski authored a series of biographical portraits of Schulz. First published in Polish under the title *Regiony wielkiej herezji*, the book was then published in English and French under the respective titles *Regions of the Great Heresy* and *Les régions de la grande hérésie;* and later translated into many other languages. As John Updike once said: what Ficowski did for Schulz's work is as significant as what Max Brot did for Kafka's. In her warm and captivating voice, Mrs. Ficowska affectionately recounted her memories of her husband's devotion to Schulz's legacy. With Mrs. Ficowska's kind permission we are including in this publication *Mon non-sauvé,* Jerzy Ficowski's poem dedicated to Bruno Schulz.

Organized by schulzophiles rather then schulzologues, our symposium's scope went beyond the academic. Each presentation was preceded by a moving interpretation of Schulz's prose by Montreal actress Liliana Komorowska. She then read corresponding excerpts from *Regions of the Great Heresy* and finally beautifully recited *Mon non-sauvé.*

The unexpected presence of Mrs. Johanna Nestel, a Holocaust survivor and a pupil of Schulz from the Drohobycz Gymnasium, created quite a sensation at our event. A filmed interview with Mrs. Nestel is included with this volume.

We are sincerely grateful to our sponsors who made this event possible. We would like to mention particularly the support of Mr. Bogdan Borusewicz, Speaker of the Senate of the Republic of Poland, professor Jerzy Wyrozumski, Secretary-General of The Polish Academy of Arts and Sciences, professor Zygmunt Kolenda from Stowarzyszenie Wspólnota Polska and Dr. Andrzej Ćwierz, member of the Diet and the President of the Polish Canadian Parliamentary Group.

Bruno Schulz: New Readings, New Meanings • Nouvelles lectures, nouvelles significations was the most important conference thus far on Bruno Schulz in North America, and we hope that the present volume will bring some new light to these new meanings, nouvelles significations.

Introduction

Stanisław Latek - Institut polonais des arts et des sciences au Canada

La présente publication est une compilation des articles présentés lors du Symposium international sur Bruno Schulz, organisé par l'Institut polonais des arts et des sciences au Canada. Cet événement, qui a eu lieu à l'université McGill à Montréal les 4 et 5 mai 2007, rassemblait des conférenciers provenant de six pays et de dix universités différentes.

Le programme du Symposium a été conçu de manière à refléter la complexité extraordinaire de l'œuvre de Schulz. Cette œuvre, malgré sa dimension périphérique, annonce les grands thèmes de l'art du 21ᵉ siècle.

En tant qu'organisateurs, nous avions voulu initialement saisir la « totalité » de l'œuvre de Schulz. Combien futile fut cette tentative, avons-nous appris plus tard lors de la Conférence d'ouverture de Jerzy Jarzębski, *Schulz: Universality and the Poetics of the Fragment,* dans laquelle celui-ci affirme : « le monde de Schulz est dominé par des visions de la réalité extérieure fragmentaire, dans tout ce qu'elle a d'inachevé et de circonstancié, et par le caractère fragmentaire du texte même. » Étant donné que si peu d'éléments de l'œuvre de Schulz ont survécu, nous sommes réduits à étudier des fragments de cette fragmentarité.

Le présent recueil s'ouvre sur un article dans lequel le nom de Bruno Schulz est à peine mentionné. En effet, le professeur Gershon Hundert, un des plus grands spécialistes de l'histoire des Juifs de Pologne et de Lituanie s'interroge sur le fait que tant de mystiques et d'artistes proviennent de Drohobycz, la ville qui sert de toile de fond à l'art de Schulz.

Dans l'article suivant, Włodzimierz Krysiński, spécialiste de la littérature comparée, confronte la prose de Schulz à celle d'une variété d'auteurs et de styles littéraires, notamment le baroque.

L'essai de Norman Ravvin offre ensuite une réflexion intéressante sur le pouvoir de mythification de l'œuvre de Schulz, et son influence sur d'autres auteurs.

De son côté, Kris Van Heuckelom analyse les thèmes idolâtres dans la prose de l'écrivain, en se concentrant sur le cycle *Manekiny* (Traité des Mannequins) issu de *Sklepy cynamonowe* (Les Boutiques de cannelle). Quant à David Goldfarb, il poursuit l'analyse du même *Traité des mannequins* en nous présentant brillamment la notion délicate de « pałuby », une notion qu'il considère indispensable à la compréhension de la littérature polonaise d'avant-guerre.

Dans son interprétation très originale de la nouvelle "Wichura" (La Bourrasque) Małgorzata Smorąg-Goldberg examine le processus de métaphorisation du langage artistique de Schulz. Elle analyse ainsi la réflexion de l'écrivain sur sa propre condition juive.

Venue directement de Drochobycz, Vira Meniok nous emmène en promenade dans la ville natale de Schulz. À travers les fragments topographiques de la ville, son voyage s'ouvre sur le cosmos. Ensuite, Maria Poprzęcka dispute les interprétations simplistes de l'œuvre visuelle de Schulz, interprétations qui ont empêché une appréciation plus complexe et complète de son œuvre.

En face de la maison familiale de l'écrivain, de l'autre côté de la Place du marché, se trouvait un cinéma appartenant à Izydor Schulz, le frère de Bruno, où celui-ci passait beaucoup de temps. C'est justement ce lien entre l'auteur et le cinéma qui est exploré par Joanne Villeneuve lorsqu'elle analyse l'influence de Schulz sur le cinéma contemporain. Sa présentation était accompagnée d'une projection de The Street of Crocodiles, un film d'animation de Stephen et Timothy Quay.

Notre invitée d'honneur était Madame Elżbieta Ficowska, veuve de feu Jerzy Ficowski, éminent poète polonais, notamment reconnu pour avoir ressuscité l'œuvre de Bruno Schulz. Jerzy Ficowski est l'auteur d'une série de portraits biographiques de Schulz. D'abord publié en polonais sous le titre *Regiony wielkiej herezji,* le livre a ensuite été publié en anglais (*Regions of the Great Heresy*), puis en français (*Les Régions de la grande hérésie*) et finalement traduit en de nombreuses autres langues. John Updike a déjà dit de Ficowski : « ce que Ficowski a fait pour l'œuvre de Schulz est aussi important que ce que Max Brot a fait pour celle de Kafka. » Dans sa voix chaude et captivante, Mme Ficowska nous a affectueusement fait part de la dévotion de son mari à l'œuvre de Schulz. C'est avec son aimable permission que nous incluons dans ce recueil *Mon non-sauvé,* le poème de Jerzy Ficowski dédié à Schulz.

Organisé par des schulzophiles plutôt que des schulzologues, notre symposium a cherché à dépasser un cadre purement académique. Chaque conférence était précédée d'une interprétation émouvante de la prose de Schulz par l'actrice montréalaise Liliana Komorowska, laquelle faisait ensuite une lecture des passages correspondants des *Régions de la grande hérésie,* et conclut finalement en récitant merveilleusement *Mon non-sauvé.*

La présence inattendue de Madame Joanna Nestel, une survivante du holocauste et une élève de Schulz du Gymnase de Drochobycz, a créé toute une sensation lors de notre évènement. Une entrevue filmée de Madame Nestel est jointe à ce recueil.

Nous aimerions remercier très sincèrement nos commanditaires, sans lesquels cet évènement n'aurait pu être possible. Nous tenons particulièrement à souligner le support de Monsieur Bogdan Borusewicz, Président du Sénat de la République de Pologne, du professeur Jerzy Wyrozumski, Secrétaire général de l'Académie polonaise des arts et des sciences, du professeur Zygmunt Kolenda de Stowarzyszenie Wspólnota Polska et de Dr. Andrzej Ćwierz, membre de la Diète et Président du groupe parlementaire Pologne-Canada.

Bruno Schulz: New Readings, New Meanings • Nouvelles lectures, nouvelles significations a été jusqu'à maintenant la conférence portant sur l'œuvre de Schulz la plus importante en Amérique du Nord. Nous espérons que le présent recueil va contribuer à propager ces nouvelles lectures et ces nouvelles significations.

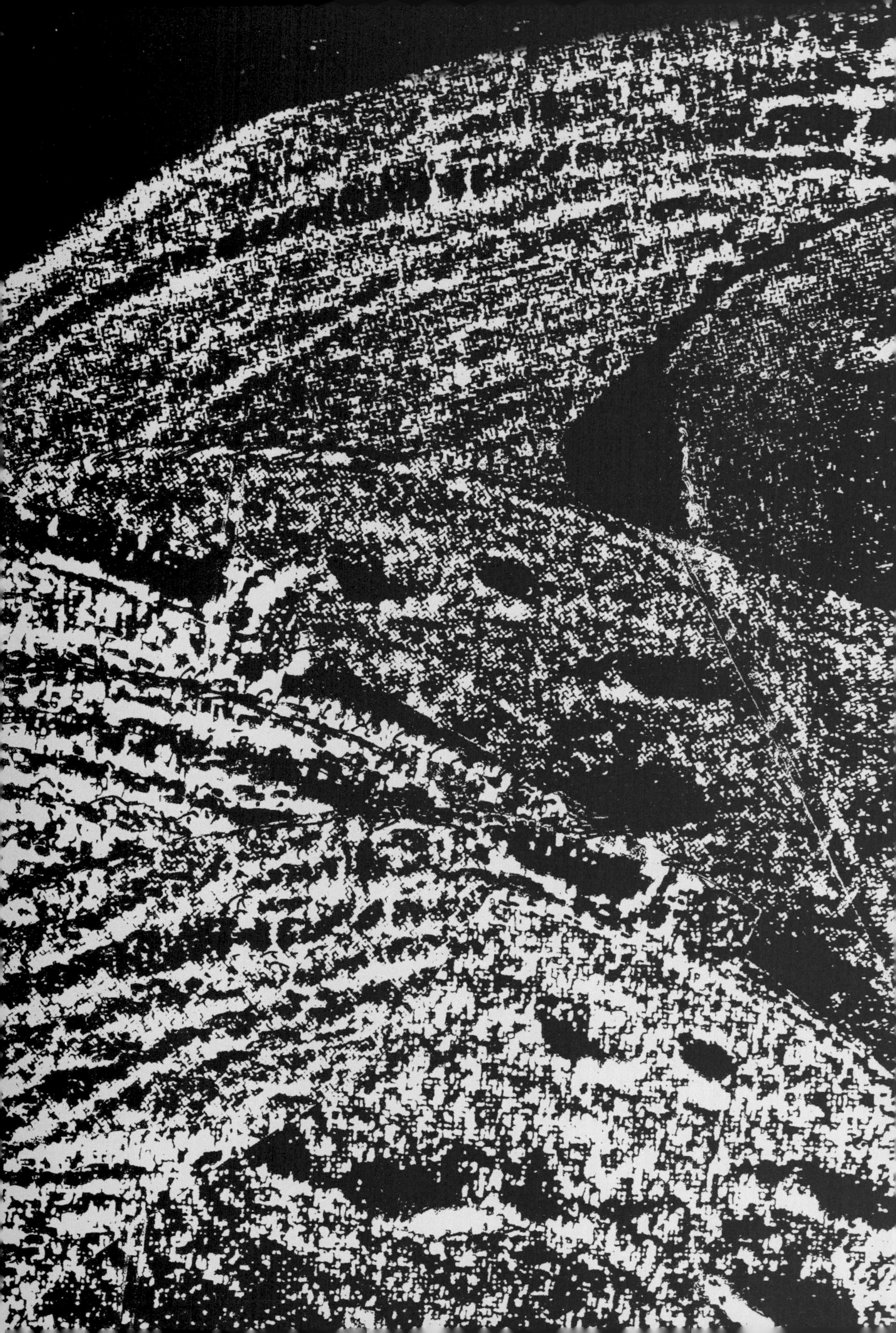

Drohobycz: City of Mystics and Artists

Gershon David Hundert – McGill University

Abstract

Some remarks on the Jewish community of Drohobycz and its history with a brief consideration of the mystics and artists produced by that community including Yentl the Prophetess, Maurycy and Leopold Gottlieb and Ephraim Moses Lilien.

My purpose in this article is to sketch some dimensions of that portion of the context in which Bruno Schulz arose that relates to the Jewish community of his native city. Although in the sixteenth century (1578) the town obtained the privilege known as *de non tolerandis Judaeis,* Jews had lived in the environs from as early as the fifteenth century. The Jewish community of Drohobycz itself was established by the end of the seventeenth century. During the eighteenth century, Jews were involved prominently in the extraction, distribution and sale of salt that was mined in the region. By 1765 the Jewish population of Drohobycz totaled 1,924, making it about 20th in relative size of contemporary Jewish communities in Poland-Lithuania.

Like all Polish-Lithuanian communities of the period, Drohobycz Jewry conducted its affairs autonomously, governed by its *kahal.* The great Galician Jewish historian Majer Bałaban studied a particular series of events related to a certain Zalman whom Bałaban styled the 'dictator of the kahal.'[1] In the middle of the 18th century a wealthy, despotic *arendarz* (farmer of the taxes and customs revenues), Zalman ben Ze'ev (Wolfowicz), enjoyed the protection of the widow of the local Starosta with whom he had a romance. With this aristocratic safeguard, he seized control of communal affairs, exploiting his position for his own financial benefit. He even appointed his son-in-law as rabbi of the community. For his ruthless treatment of both Jews and non-Jews he was finally denounced to the authorities by an unusual coalition of Jews and Christians; in 1755 he was arrested, tried, and condemned to death, but as generous assistance was contributed by his coreligionists, the sentence was commuted to life imprisonment. After about a year in prison he adopted Christianity and died a member of the Carmelite order in 1757. There is a

1 Polish version: *Nasz kraj* (Styczeń, 1909); *Dziennik Polski* (Lemberg 1909), nr. 38–51 and in M. Bałaban, *Z historii Żydów w Polsce,* 129–146; Hebrew: *Ha-tsefira,* no. 265–268; Yiddish: *Nayer Haynt* 1926, nr. 31, 43, 55 and *Yidn in Poyln* (Vilna: Kletzkin, 1930), 67–87.

Ukrainian folksong, still sung at Easter in the interwar period that recalls this story: *Nye panuye Zalman.*

Beginning in the late seventeenth century, the penetration of kabbalah and kabbalistic ideas altered the very grammar of Jewish culture in eastern Europe and elsewhere.[2] These mystical trends and systems of thought stemmed largely from a galaxy of mystics and theologians who were concentrated in the town of Safed in the Galilee in the sixteenth century. It is not possible here to present a synthetic summary of these ideas and metaphysical systems.[3] One such school, called Lurianic after Isaac Luria (d. 1572) focuses on the human role in accelerating the progress toward redemption and the arrival of the Messiah. It should not be surprising then that early in the eighteenth century two types of religious figures became prominent. One group was called pietists (*khsidim*). They were pious, learned, ascetic and elitist. Generally, a few such men in each community prayed separately using a mystical liturgy. They enjoyed respect but had little connection to the community at large. Note that these are "old style" *khsidim,* not the same as those who arose in the wake of Israel Baal Shem Tov in the last quarter of the eighteenth century and are also called Hasidim. A second group can accurately be referred to as shamans, called *ba`alei shem or ba`alei shem tov.* They were sometimes called kabbalists (*mekubalim*) and here one should keep in mind that the boundary between mysticism and magic was not hard and fast.

In Drohobycz in the early 18th century there was a figure of this kind known as Yosef Virnik, called Spravidliver by Polish speakers in the town. Abraham Joshua Heschel translated the term "spravidliver" to mean truthful.[4] In my opinion a better translation of sprawiedliwy would be "just", *i.e.* the *tsaddik!* His wife was called Yente or Yentl the prophetess. It was said that she could hear the angels singing. Their son, Isaak or Yitshak of Drohobycz (by ca 1695) was a well-known kabbalist and *baal shem.* For a time, he belonged to a conventicler of kabbalists (*kloyz*) in Ostróg, and later lived for a period in

2 See Gershon David Hundert, *Jews in Poland-Lithuania in the 18th Century: A Genealogy of Modernity,* University of California Press, Berkeley, California, 2004, 119–130 or *idem, Żydzi w Rzeczypospolitej Obojga Narodów w XVIII wieku: Genealogia nowoczesności,* Cyklady, Warszawa, 2007, 160–174.

3 See Gershom Scholem, *Major trends in Jewish mysticism,* Schocken Books, New York, 1995; po polsku: *Mistycyzm żydowski i jego główne kierunki,* przełożył Ireneusz Ania, Czytelnik, Warszawa, 1997.

4 *The Circle of the Baal Shem Tov: Studies in Hasidism,* ed. Samuel H. Dresner, University of Chicago Press, Chicago, 1985, 153–157, 166–167.

Brody. Isaac was known for his particular ability to save souls trapped in the hellish chains of transmigration and reincarnation. His son was Yekhi'el Mikhl of Zloczew, one of the most important leaders of the Hasidic movement that emerged in the 1760's. Known as the *maggid* of Złoczów, he established his own community of followers which, in this case, was an elite brotherhood that was a continuation in many ways of the pattern of the old-style *khsidim.*[5]

Through the nineteenth and the first decades of the twentieth century, Drohobycz was a center of Ukrainian Hasidism. Particularly important were the groups of followers of Rizhin-Sadagora and Boyaner Hasidism.[6] In fact, Hasidim may have made up the majority of the city's 8,055 Jews who, by 1869, constituted the largest single ethnic-religious group in this tri-ethnic town – 47% of the total population. Ukrainians (29%) and Poles (23%) made up the rest.[7] It was a typical Galician Jewish community except for one dimension. That is, the existence there, from the mid-nineteenth century, of an important oil industry.

The first attempts to prospect for oil and its extraction were made in Drohobycz early in the nineteenth century and eventually a refinery was constructed by Abraham Schreiner in nearby Borysław at the same time as the industry was developing in the United States. After many failures, Schreiner succeeded in establishing the first petroleum refinery in Borysław in 1854. Many railway companies then ordered petroleum from him for lighting their carriages and stations. Thus he became one of the world's first "petroleum kings" until the destruction of his refinery in a fire in 1886. Drohobycz Jews took a prominent part in oil extraction and refining, and its export was mainly in Jewish hands. Many families made fortunes in this sector. The take-over of the smaller companies by big enterprises at the end of the 19th century, however, badly hit the Jewish concerns, and the economic position of the community began to deteriorate.

---

[5] See the claims advanced by Mor Altshuler, "Mishnato shel R. Mehullam Feibush Heller umekomah bereshit hatenu`ah hahassidit," (Ph.D. diss., Hebrew University, 1994), and in *The Messianic Secret of Hasidism,* Brill, Leiden and Boston, 2006; Heschel, *The Circle of the Baal Shem Tov,* idem., pp. 178–181.

[6] See David Assaf, *The Regal Way: The Life and Times of Rabbi Israel of Ruzhin,* translated from Hebrew by David Louvish, Stanford University Press, Stanford, 2002.

[7] The Jewish population was 8,683 in 1900, and 11,833 (about 44% of the total population) in 1921. In 1874, the Drohobycz town council was composed of eight Poles, twelve Ruthenians and sixteen Jews. From then until World War II, a Jew was always elected Deputy Mayor of Drohobycz.

It turns out that there is a Canadian dimension to the squeezing out of Jews from the petroleum industry. Canadian entrepreneur W. H. MacGarvey helped develop the rig in the 1860's or 70's which made Canadian drilling technology and Canadian drillers famous around the world. MacGarvey came to Galicia in 1883 and a year later was able to bore holes of 700 to 1000 metres. By 1904 there were thirty boreholes in Borysław of over 1000 meters. MacGarvey established a company called MacGarvey and Bergheim, later known as the 'Galizische-Karpaten Naptha AG' and made a fortune from his Galician properties. The oil derricks of Galicia were big wooden structures of the so-called Canadian-Polish type, for the Canadian engineers who were hired to supervise field development. To protect workers from cold, wind and snow during the harsh local winters, derricks featured wooden walls with windows and were equipped with a central heating system using steam. The pyramidal towers were usually around 25 m (80 feet) high and often included a pump to lift the oil from the 1400-1500 m (4500-5000 feet) deep wells.

Of course the Jewish community of Drohobycz, particularly in light of the wealth of the community, soon came to include modernizers as well as *khsidim*. We have a colourful description of the community on the eve of World War I from the pen of David Horowitz, a founder of left-wing Zionism (Hashomer Hatsa`ir) and later a senior bureaucrat in the State of Israel:

> Drohobycz was, so far as social life in the small towns of Galicia is concerned, an exceptional case. On the surface it was like all other such places: melancholy, and a gloomy atmosphere of hopelessness, reigned. All the usual elements of Galician society were present: hasids and enlightened Jews, an intelligentsia looking with curious astonishment both to the east and to the west, assimilationists entranced by the charms of foreign culture, signs of an emerging Zionist movement, liberals and conservatives, religious functionaries and merchants, rich and poor. And yet it was different, all these various elements within society had more energy than elsewhere, the pace was faster. Everything was somehow sharper, more varied, more conspicuous. It was clear that there was more drive and ferment here than in other Galician cities. The oil emerging from the ground in the neighbouring small town of Borysław created social and economic change unknown elsewhere... This was the only town in Galicia

> that attracted international attention. Here great opportunities for easy wealth opened up. The nouveaux riches owed their wealth to this inflammable substance, to the liquid that was in demand all over the world, that made possible the transportation and factory systems of the economy. Life in Drohobycz was like life in a hot swamp. Rottenness and a bad smell were everywhere. Intrigue and gambling, adultery, vast social differentiation, easy and quick enrichment, all this was common to the broad stratum of the newly wealthy. The race for the liquid gold stamped itself on all aspects of life. And along with all this, among the young intelligentsia, there was quite a different atmosphere – disgust with the pursuit of money, repulsion from the cynicism and the constant pursuit of wealth, from the seekers after gold, from the provincial Jewish Klondike of the small Galician town.[8]

Because it was the center of the oil industry, Drohobycz was home to the third wealthiest Jewish community in Galicia after Lwów and Kraków. The unstable but significant wealth of the town, the mixture of mysticism and modernizing and, perhaps, the aroma of crude oil, combined with whatever mysterious forces were at work in the eastern part of Galicia to make Drohobycz produce a series of important Jewish artists. I should like to discuss two of them, very briefly.

In the Muzeum Narodowe in Warsaw, one of the most visited rooms contains Jan Matejko's *The Battle at Grunwald.* Directly opposite that painting hangs Maurycy Gottlieb's work *Christ Preaching at Capernaum.* In the Tel Aviv Museum, one of the main attractions is Gottlieb's *Jews Praying on the Day of Atonement.* Both paintings - Matejko's and Gottlieb's - were completed in 1878 and both have become iconic and canonical.

Maurycy Gottlieb (1856-1879), whose life ended before he reached the age of 30, nonetheless produced a number of works that continue to be reproduced and exhibited frequently.[9] He was the son of a prosperous owner of an oil refinery. Under the influence of his teacher at the Cracow Academy, Jan

---

8 David Horowitz, *Ha-etmol sheli* (Jerusalem, 1970), 13–14. Translation follows Ezra Mendelsohn, *Painting a People: Maurycy Gottlieb and Jewish Art,* Brandeis University Press, Hanover NH and London, 2002, 20.

9 What follows is based on ibid., Ezra Mendelsohn, *Painting a People.*

Matejko, Gottlieb turned from German to Polish subject matter. Gottlieb was subjected to anti-Semitic taunts, and painted a self-portrait called "Ahasuerus," which referred to the legend of the Wandering Jew who was shunned by everyone. In 1876 he received a prize at Munich for his painting, "Shylock and Jessica." The noted publisher Bruckmann then commissioned him to make twelve illustrations for a deluxe edition of Gotthold Ephraim Lessing's drama *Nathan der Weise.* Yielding to anti-Semitic pressure, Bruckmann canceled the commission after seven of the illustrations had been finished. Gottlieb's next major work, "Jews praying on the Day of Atonement," was stimulated by his studying Heinrich Graetz' *Geschichte der Juden.* The picture caused a sensation in Jewish circles, and the Jewish press hailed it as a genuinely Jewish masterpiece. With the aid of a Viennese patron, Gottlieb went to Rome, where he again met his teacher Matejko, who greeted him as "the most hopeful disciple of Polish art, whom I greet as my successor." After a few months in Rome, Gottlieb went back to Cracow, where he died at the age of 23. Considering the fact that Gottlieb's career covered only four or five years, his extant work is remarkable both in quality and quantity. "Shylock and Jessica" is so well and richly painted that the theatricality of the scene is overlooked, and "Jews Praying on the Day of Atonement" (which embodies a self-portrait) is an indisputable masterpiece. Gottlieb was also an excellent portraitist. His portraits are gems of psychological penetration in an era that often beautified and falsified its sitters. His portraits of girls and elderly women have delicacy, lightness of touch, and charm.

Maurycy's younger brother Leopold Gottlieb (1883–1934), the 13th child of the Gottlieb family, studied in Cracow, Munich, and Paris, and for a while taught at the Bezalel School in Jerusalem. During World War I he was a lieutenant in the Polish Legion, and thereafter fought under Piłsudski in Poland's War of Independence. Among the numerous personalities who sat for him for portraits were Piłsudski and the writer Sholem Asch.

Finally, there is another Jewish son of Drohobycz who also studied with Matejko, although rather briefly, and whose art also became widely known. Ephraim Moses Lilien (1874–1925), became, one might say, the first iconographer of Zionism.[10] He took an active part in three consecutive Zionist Congresses and was a member of the Democratic Fraction, which stressed

10 What follows on Lilien is based on Michael Stanislawski, *Zionism and the Fin de Siècle: Cosmopolitanism and Nationalism from Nordau to Jabotinsky,* University of California Press, Berkeley, California, 2001.

the need to foster Jewish culture. He was one of the founders of the Berlin publishing house, *Jüdischer Verlag*, which he served not only as an illustrator but also as editor, manager, and publicity agent. He collaborated closely with Theodor Herzl; Lilien's photograph of the Zionist leader on the Rhine Bridge, his Herzl portraits, and his decorations for the Golden Book of the Jewish National Fund became familiar to Zionists all over the world. In 1905 Lilien, along with Boris Schatz and others, was a member of the committee formed to establish the Bezalel School of Art in Jerusalem. He taught there for some months in the following year and revisited Palestine three times, on the last occasion as a lieutenant in the Austro-Hungarian army during World War I.

In 1908 Lilien turned from book illustration to etching. Many of his etchings are views of Austria and Hungary, while others record his impressions of Palestine, Damascus, and Beirut. His drawings, executed mainly in India ink, show a crisp, elegant line and a strong contrast between black and white areas. Ephraim Moses Lilien was also the "father of Jewish bookplates." He designed many for early Zionist leaders which revealed national suffering and hopes. In all his work, any scene of ancient Judea was illustrated by Lilien in a highly ornamental and sensualist orientalist fashion, stressing the physical beauty and sculptured bodies, male and female, of the ancient Israelites. The Jew of the Exile, by contrast, was depicted as an old, sad, bearded and bedraggled Orthodox Jew, usually surrounded by thorns or even barbed wire.

I offer no solution to the conundrum of what it was about Drohobycz that made it home to so many artistic temperaments (and certainly not only Jews – one might mention Ivan Franko [1856-1916] here as well). The theme of exile, however, physical and psychological, surely is part of the story along with the mysticism of the Hasidim and the aroma of crude oil.

Schulz et le baroque. L'herméneutique différentielle et le savoir sectionné

Włodzimierz Krysiński – Université de Montréal

Resumé

A l'origine de ma démarche critique il y a une hypothèse de travail : l'approche comparative devrait faciliter l'approfondissement de la connaissance de l'oeuvre de Schulz. Connaître Schulz comparativement signifie, en premier lieu, fixer différents champs de comparabilités comprises comme confrontation de ses spécifités thématiques et formelles avec certains univers narratifs et certain types particuliers de la représentation littéraire.

En second lieu, la saisie comparative de l'univers de Schulz devrait chercher a établir ses liens avec certains styles littéraires, comme le baroque et l'expressionnisme, afin de pénétrer dans ce qui est irréductible et propre a Schulz.

Certaines dynamiques narratives du XXe siècle (Kafka, Musil, Döblin, Proust, Pirandello, Joyce, Borges, Cortázar) projetées sur l'oeuvre de Schulz devraient nous permettre de définir son originalité exceptionnelle qui, semble-t-il, réside bien plus dans une combinaison d'éléments disparates que dans une invention du nouveau absolu.

L'œuvre de Bruno Schulz a été scrutée de fond en comble et, semble-t-il, rien de nouveau sous ce soleil ne pourrait plus advenir. Et pourtant… L'histoire de la critique de cette oeuvre a tout d'abord enregistré une série d'études ponctuelles et générales portant sur certains aspects de l'œuvre (*La phénoménologie du rêve dans la prose de Bruno Schulz* par M. Rabizo-Birek ; *La réalité dégradée* par A. Sandauer ; *La faillite du réel chez Bruno Schulz* par J. Speina[1]) pour finalement aboutir à des approches encyclopédiques.

La schulzologia (schulzologie) s'est développée comme une sorte d'herméneutique différentielle qui d'une façon naturelle a donné lieu à une division du travail. Le couronnement de cette progression est le *Słownik schulzowski*

[1] M. Rabizo-Birek, *Fenomenologia marzenia w prozie Brunona Schulza* (La phénoménologie du rêve dans la prose de Bruno Schulz) dans *W stronę dwudziestolecia 1918–1939. Studia i szkice o literaturze,* ed. Z. Andres, Wydawnictwo Wyższej Szkoły Pedagogicznej, Rzeszów, 1993 ; A. Sandauer, *Rzeczywistość zdegradowana (Rzecz o Brunonie Schulzu)* (La réalité dégradée) dans *Zebrane pisma krytyczne,* Państwowy Instytut Wydawniczy, Warszawa, 1981, v. 1, pp. 557–580 ; J. Speina, *Bankructwo realności. Proza Brunona Schulza,* (La faillite du réel chez Bruno Schulz), Państwowe Wydawnictwo Naukowe, Warszawa–Poznań, 1974.

ou *Dictionnaire de Schulz*[2], travail collectif dont les différentes entrées ont été confiées à des spécialistes. La table des matières de ce dictionnaire révèle différents aspects qu'on peut résumer de la manière suivante : 1. Biographie très détaillée de Schulz ; celle-ci fait état des personnes qui ont joué un rôle particulier dans la vie de l'écrivain ; 2. Répertoire thématique et critique de l'œuvre : *autokastracja* (autocastration), *bestiarium* (bestiaire), *bestie* (bêtes), *czarny pies* (chien noir). En outre, le *Dictionnaire* énumère et définit certains termes ou concepts qui ont une portée métacritique: *awangardowość, groteska, ironia, symbol, poezja, symbolizm, tekst, tragiczność.* La dissection encyclopédique de l'œuvre constitue une sorte de leçon d'anatomie dont le Professeur Tulp est invisible, mais dont les participants expliquent individuellement les éléments constitutifs du corps exposé aux regards des chirurgiens. Les très nombreux détails se superposent et dépassent la qualité physio-intellectuelle du créateur. La finitude du corps, son anatomie disséquée dans ses moindres éléments créent une illusion de complétude. Ce corps a vécu, ce corps a parlé, ce corps a pensé. Cette anatomie a aimé. Elle a été une façon d'approcher la métaphysique, la pensée et les fantasmes que le sujet Schulz a expérimentés. Le savoir encyclopédique sectionne l'œuvre en éléments fonctionnels, mais pas nécessairement solidaires. Potentiellement, chaque entrée est dotée d'une dynamique qui présuppose un parcours de l'œuvre dont les finalités peuvent varier. Ainsi, une sorte de tension se produit entre l'écriture de Schulz et ses composantes individuelles. L'écriture est une synthèse dynamique qui d'une façon syncrétique unit aussi bien la modulation énonciative et stylistique que l'oscillation entre le subjectif et le normatif. La lecture et l'interprétation de l'œuvre de Schulz qui se dégagent du *Dictionnaire* sont partiellement orientées et reflètent la tension évoquée plus haut entre les éléments individuels et le processus d'écriture.

L'apparente exhaustivité de la matière critique du *Dictionnaire* fait place nolens volens à de nouvelles visions relativisantes. Prenons l'exemple du baroque. C'est un des éléments caractéristiques des modalités de la représentation dans l'œuvre de Schulz.

Modalités du baroque chez Schulz

Voici un rappel du terme de baroque présent dans l'œuvre de Schulz. L'écrivain mentionne des « prospectus baroques » comme manifestation d'un style et

[2] *Słownik schulzowski* [Dictionnaire de Schulz], eds. W. Bolecki, J. Jarzębski, S. Rosiek, Słowo/Obraz/Terytoria, n.d. Gdańsk, 2003.

comme modalité d'indiquer quelque chose qui en soi ne se laisse pas voir de façon claire. Ainsi, les environs de la rue des Crocodiles font une « tache blanche » qui est comparable à celle qui signale les régions polaires ou les pays incertains ou inexplorés. Schulz choisit le style des « prospectus baroques » afin de signifier une réalité incertaine des pays comparables aux régions polaires et aux pays « incertains ou inexplorés ». Dans « La rue des crocodiles » le passage suivant exprime ainsi la fonction spécifique du style baroque :

> Or, sur ce plan dessiné dans le style des prospectus baroques, les environs de la rue des Crocodiles faisaient une tache blanche comparable à celle qui, dans les géographies, signale les régions polaires, les pays incertains ou inexplorés[3].

Il y a chez Schulz une conscience du baroque. Et cette conscience facilite l'utilisation de ses différentes modalité dans l'écriture qui se tourne vers l'espace et vers l'atmosphère que l'écrivain connaît bien, mais qu'il tient à montrer comme différentes représentations du microcosme de la ville, de la région, des rêves et des impressions, des fantasmes et des illusions qui font partie de son vécu de l'étrangeté. Car c'est justement cette donnée essentielle qui est la mesure du monde et l'inspiration définitive de l'écrivain.

La question du baroque dans l'œuvre de Schulz relève du fait que son écriture exhibe une considérable polysémie formelle et une construction stylistique qui différencient ses messages sémantiques. Ce que Schulz communique est susceptible d'interprétations dont l'éventail est très large. Toutefois, son microcosme se fonde sur une perception systématique de l'étrangeté et sur une expansion de sa vision. L'étrangeté comprise au sens d'*Unheimliche,* telle que Freud l'explique, montre le monde décrit comme un « locus suspectus », comme un « lieu suspect ». Cette communication de l'étrangeté présuppose des nuances dans la transmission de la vision. Et c'est ainsi que le baroque entre en ligne de compte. Il est un paramètre stylistique qui permet de rendre fonctionnelles et esthétiquement pregnantes la diversité et la dynamique de l'écriture. Le baroque s'y installe comme trois perspectives d'intensité des visions narrativisées. Appelons-les respectivement : 1) coloration baroque ; 2) accentuation baroque ; 3) déformation baroque. Nous allons essayer de montrer comment ces trois degrés d'intensité caractérisent l'œuvre de Schulz.

[3] B. Schulz, « La rue des Crocodiles », dans *Les boutiques de cannelle,* tr. G. Sidre, Denoël, Paris, 1974, p. 116.

Rappelons d'abord les traits saillants du baroque classique et du baroque moderne dont la présence dans l'écriture romanesque ou dans la poésie est un fait reconnu par la critique littéraire. Le baroque classique (Gongora, Quevedo, Marino, Sęp-Szarzynski) est un art d'ornement. C'est un style flamboyant et hypermétaphorique. Le monde ainsi exprimé est une création de formes baroquisantes comprises comme style flamboyant et ornemental. Il est évident que Schulz ne pratique pas ce genre de baroque. L'écriture de Schulz ne va pas dans cette direction. Elle dépasse le baroque classique des métaphores luxuriantes où le monde est représenté comme une structure impénétrable et jamais totalement descriptible. Pour Schulz, en revanche, le baroque est un support formel qui participe à une dialectique de la représentation du monde car celle-ci procède sélectivement : la localisation et la saisie de lieux à narrer, une approche stylistique de l'objet à décrire et le parachèvement de la narration ou du discours qui nomme, pénètre et montre l'objet.

Visions modernes du baroque

Le baroque moderne, fortement marqué dans le domaine littéraire latino-américain, se caractérise par « le décentrement, la prolifération, le mouvement. Ce qui s'oppose au classicisme, à l'ordre, à la symétrie, à la stabilité, à la mesure » constate Guy Scarpetta[4].

Pour Alejo Carpentier « le baroque est un style dans lequel, tout autour de l'axe central… se multiplient ce que nous pourrions appeler les noyaux proliférants » (focos proliferantes), c'est-à-dire des éléments décoratifs qui remplissent entièrement l'espace de la construction[5]. Le philosophe français G. Deleuze a théorisé le baroque d'une façon originale et fonctionnelle :

Le baroque ne renvoie pas à une essence, mais plutôt à une fonction opératoire, à un trait. Il ne cesse de faire des plis (…) il courbe et recourbe les plis, les pousse à l'infini, pli sur pli, pli selon le pli. Le trait du Baroque, c'est le pli qui va à l'infini. Et d'abord il les différencie suivant deux directions, suivant deux infinis, comme si l'infini avait deux étages : les replis de la matière, et le pli dans l'âme[6].

La façon dont Deleuze comprend le récit baroque ouvre une voie d'investigation sur le baroque de Schulz. Deleuze constate : « Le Baroque introduit un

[4] G. Scarpetta, *L'Artifice,* Grasset, Paris, 1988, p. 18.

[5] A. Carpentier, *L'Eternel retour du baroquisme* dans *Magazine littéraire, L'âge baroque,* no. 300, juin 1992, p. 28

[6] G. Deleuze, *Le pli : Leibniz et le baroque,* Minuit, Paris, 1988, p. 5

nouveau type de récit où... la description prend la place de l'objet, le concept devient narratif, et le sujet, point de vue, sujet d'énonciation »[7]. Ce constat de Deleuze aide à mettre en relief le fait que ce que nous avons appelé les trois degrés d'intensité et de particularité de la prose de Schulz : la coloration, l'accentuation et la déformation baroques participent à la création d'un type de récit où la description remplace l'objet, le concept se transforme en une structure narrative, le sujet, ainsi que le point deviennent sujet d'énonciation.

La question de la généalogie du baroque, telle que nous la comprenons est liée à la question de la langue. Celle-ci a été maintes fois étudiée. Référons-nous aux observations pertinentes de Jerzy Jarzębski :

> Schulz appartient à ces créateurs qui modélisent avec art et d'une façon spécifique le langage de leurs messages ; il est alors impossible de ne pas apercevoir sa particularité. Déjà les premiers critiques de *Boutiques de cannelle* soulignaient la richesse et l'excentricité du vocabulaire, la poésie particulière, un peu maniérée de ses « indifférences », « conglomérats », « gynocraties », « antécédents », etc. inscrits dans le récit dont les sujets étaient prosaïques ou tout simplement vulgaires[8].

En citant quelques fragments des *Boutiques de cannelle,* Jarzębski synthétise avec justesse ses observations :

> On voit qu'il y a ici certaines images métaphoriques plus grandes qui groupent autour d'elles le vocabulaire propre à un domaine spécifique (microbiologie, géographie, astronomie ou botanique), ensuite de cette matière verbale se dégage une nouvelle image dont les métaphores se mêlent, et finalement les opérations stylistiques produisent une interpénétration des sphères de la réalité, « déplacent le ciel sur la terre » et tout ce procès culmine sous forme d'un événement fantastique « les hommes ramassent les étoiles tombantes »[9].

[7] ibid., p. 174.

[8] J. Jarzębski, *Wstęp* [Introduction] dans B. Schulz, *Opowiadania. Wybór Esejów i Listów* [Récits, Choix d'Essais et de Lettres], Zakład Narodowy Imienia Ossolinskich, Wrocław et Kraków, 1989, p. XXXI

[9] ibid., p. XXXII

En suivant la voie de Jarzębski on voit que la réalité représentée par Schulz se caractérise par une sorte de tectonique verbale où les termes recherchés et superposés fondent une vision baroque comprise comme un kaléidoscope en mouvement permanent. Paradoxalement, ce même kaléidoscope ralentit et devient une sorte de grand microscope qui permet au narrateur de tout voir. Le lecteur est entré dans la tragi-comédie du spectacle baroque infini, mais tactiquement dosé par l'écrivain. L'option baroquisante crée un nouveau langage : poétique, mi-narratif, mi-discursif, sensible aux formes et aux métaphores. Ce langage signale et produit une coloration baroque. Voici un exemple :

> La nuit de juillet ! Fluide, énigmatique de l'ombre, matière vivante des ténèbres, vive, mobile, vigilante et qui tire du chaos une foule de formes aussitôt délaissées ! Matériau noir qui amoncelle autour du visiteur engourdi grottes, voûtes et portiques ! Tel le bavard importun, elle ne quitte plus l'exploration solitaire , mais l'enclôt vite dans le circuit de ses spectres, ne cessant de créer, d'inventer des fantasmes, des divagations toujours nouvelles, jamais lasse d'halluciner le voyageur de ses lointains étoilés, de ses voies lactées, de ses labyrinthes sans fin que prolongent les colisées et les forums[10].

La séquence narrative se transforme en discours et les éléments accentués par le narrateur fondent une scène cosmologique où se superposent tectoniquement les signes saisis par le narrateur : grottes, voûtes, portiques, spectres, fantasmes, « des divagations toujours nouvelles », labyrinthes sans fin. Voici Monsieur Charles qui plonge oniriquement dans un univers étrange, dont les formes et l'aura l'envahissent et le transforment :

> A tâtons, dans l'obscurité, il s'enfonçait dans des montagnes blanchâtres, des chaînes et des amoncellements de plumes fraîches, et il s'endormait ainsi, sens dessus dessous, à l'envers, la tête en bas enfoncée dans la douce chair de l'édredon, comme s'il voulait traverser en dormant les massifs puissants

10 B. Schulz, « La nuit de juillet » dans *Le sanatorium au croque-mort,* tr. A. Kosko, Denoël, Paris, 1974, p. ww125.

> de literie qui grandissaient la nuit. Il luttait avec eux dans son sommeil, nageur combattant avec l'eau[11];

Le baroque logé dans cette narration est aussi de l'ordre de l'accentuation. Il montre la puissance transformatrice de l'énergie nocturne, car une fois tous les accents mis sur les signes sélectionnés par le narrateur, son débit identifie et fixe le parcours de la nuit qui se montre comme une puissance déformatrice de son statut imaginaire. Le cosmos subit une transformation notable. Il est protéïforme :

> L'air nocturne est cet obscur Protée habile à susciter par simple jeu de riches condensations de velours, des bouffées de jasmin odorant, des cascades d'ozone, puis de brusques déserts sans souffle, ces grands bulbes noirs qui prolifèrent à l'infini, monstrueuses grappes de ténèbres gonflées de jus ombreux. Je me faufile à travers ces étroites corniches, je courbe le chef sous ces arcades, ces cryptes et ces voûtes basses et voilà que tout à coup le plafond se rompt, s'arrête dans un soupir étoilé, entrebâille l'abîme de son ciel immense pour me ramener derechef dans le dédale resserré de ses corniches et de ses couloirs[12].

Le baroque joue à plein la déformation du sensuel et du visible. Le poétique et le fictionnel aident le narrateur à identifier la nuit et à la nommer au-delà de la coloration et de l'accentuation. La transformation et la déformation créent une perspective de relativisation de ce théâtre des premiers signes du baroque où la coloration et l'accentuation entrent dans le jeu de l'écriture. C'est le triomphe de la force irrépressible de l'identité nocturne, unique et finalement nommée.

Le baroque est, chez Schulz, une forme de connaissance qui se laisse saisir et apprécier par la gradation et la différenciation du langage, par la marche accumulative du verbe. Entre le style qui, d'une part, colore de façon baroque la description du visible et de l'imaginaire ainsi que l'originalité des formes du nocturne et, d'autre part, le style qui accentue certains éléments saillants

---

11 B. Schulz, *Monsieur Charles* dans *Les boutiques de cannelle,* tr. T. Douchy, Denoël, Paris, 1974, p. 97.

12 B. Schulz, *La nuit de juillet,* op. cit., p. 125–126.

présents dans le regard de plus en plus pénétrant du narrateur, s'établit une solidarité cognitive et mimétique.

La narration chez Schulz est baroque de façon moderne puisqu'elle construit le même théâtre de l'expression du visible et de l'immaginable que certains écrivains vont pratiquer après Schulz : Alejo Carpentier, José Lezama Lima, Joao Guimares Rosa. La puissance poétique et expressionniste du discours de Schulz produit des visions baroques, les plus aptes à ancrer sa vision du monde constamment médiatisée par le jeu de fantasmes et de formes qui marquent la force de son imagination riche et souple qui s'ajuste au réel observé et fantasmagorique. Toutefois, celle-ci est capable de mesurer la distance entre son inventivité imaginaire, verbale et la permanence existentielle et théâtrale des personnages qui peuplent ses spectacles : le père, les mannequins, le retraité, Jojo, Dodo, Monsieur Charles, la solitude. Cette distance ne sera jamais transgressée au détriment de ces êtres et de ces problèmes. La structure profonde de l'œuvre de Schulz s'appuie sur un équilibre. Le baroque de Schulz n'est jamais débridé. Ici, il montre ses limites : il n'est ni inépuisable ni insondable. Il est fonctionnel par rapport à l'étrangeté du monde. Son instrumentalité s'arrête là où le regard de Schulz ne s'imagine plus trouver un autre cosmos rempli d'autres êtres baroques ou pseudo-baroques.

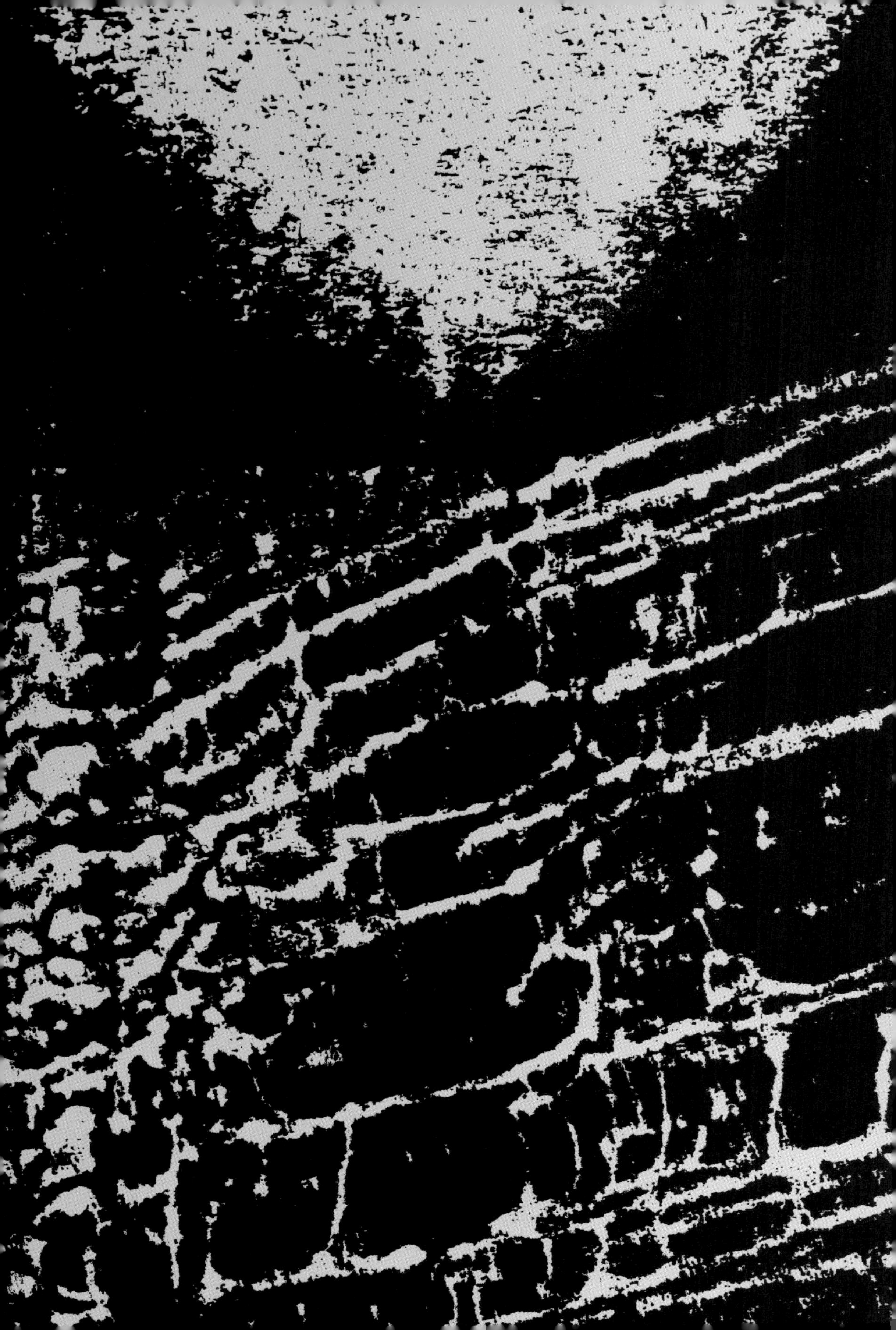

Schulz: Universality and the Poetics of the Fragment

JERZY JARZĘBSKI – Jagiellonian University

Abstract

In studies pertaining to Schulz's work, it became customary to treat his stories as elements of a grand Whole constituting a certain world order, remarkably consistent in its assumptions, embracing conceptions of physical reality, space and time, as well as language and metaphysics. Hitherto, these studies had variously emphasized one or another aspect of that Whole, giving it a different appearance in the interpretations produced by such observers as Sandauer, Speina, Panas or the undersigned. However, the hypothesis of universalism remained dominant. Even incidental observations regarding the various references and interpretative peculiarities of Schulz, show regard for that holistic perspective, which leads to an impression that this author of merely two books and only a few loose stories and essays, seems to be one of the most universal artists of Polish, and perhaps of world literature. Discovered among his stories were insights from psychology, sociology, economics, as well as a paraphrasing of modern history, and even a treatise on the nature of scientific discoveries, artistic creativity, extending also to Divine creation. His metaphors reveal sense-generating functions, and his symbolisms were to relate to great religions and human mythologies.

At the same time a striking feature of the output of the author of Cinnamon Shops seems to be his poetry of a fragment: a momentary flash... transitory, incomplete, defective; an interrupted, unrealised plot. His uses of banal clichés in a description of the world, the use of contrived mannequins instead of humans, and so on — are equally striking. This bizarre contradiction pervades Schulz's entire creative œuvre, determines its ironic character, conveying the deeply rooted inadequacy of the human individual, who nonetheless is compelled to deal with the world as a Whole, remaining a mere speck of matter, which imprisons the mind, ever too weak for the tasks it confronts. This contradiction is characteristic of the fears and disappointments in the thinking of the 20th century, and shows Schulz as a typical artist and thinker of his time.

A widely accepted reading of Bruno Schulz treats him in reference to a much wider culture. His stories are viewed as fragments referring us to some unifying concept of space, time, humankind, divinity, creativity, sexuality, etc. – the list goes on and on. I mention this interpretative practice as someone who has contributed to it; in a paper prepared for the 1992 centenary conference on Schulz in Kraków, I went so far as to say:

What we know about these stories is that they constitute a mere fragment of a hypothetical Whole; each of the texts finds its own place within this Whole; none can function separately, without reference to the others. Schulz's writing resembles Mendeleev's periodic table, which offers a holistic and inherently ordered vision of the world, even if we might not know all its constituent elements. Unlike chemistry, however, literature does not know the limits that would allow us to complete this vast structure; it does not provide the observer with any precise map of 'blank spaces' to be charted. Therefore, new texts might easily be added to the Schulz canon or subtracted from it, but such practices would not affect its comprehensive vision of the world, which rests not so much on (rather feeble) plot developments, but on the integrity of mythic time and space; on the concept of humankind, of demiurgy; on the relations between matter and spirit, femininity and masculinity, chaos and order, and so forth – in short, on certain general premises concerning the nature of Being.[1]

Similarly, other scholars have often spoken about Schulz as a creator of a holistic vision of the universe. Sandauer's reading, for example, took advantage of a broadly understood 'myth of defeat,' with its psychological, erotic, national, social, economic and artistic aspects, which he associated with Schulz's masochistic tendencies.[2] Władysław Panas has used the symbolic and conceptual grid borrowed from Isaac Luria's Kabbalah,[3] by which he sought to explicate not only the dynamics of the world's transformations, but also the particularities of Schulz's imagery. My own investigations have concentrated on reconstructing a spatial and temporal order and, within it, on locating the elements of chaos and disorder that reflected what was unclear, problematic, and instinctive in a human being, which, in turn, mirrored the dynamics of

1 J. Jarzębski, „Spojrzenie w przyszłość" in *Prowincja Centrum. Przypisy do Schulza* [A Look into the Future, Province Centre. Annotating Schulz], Wydawnictwo Literackie, Kraków, 2005, pp. 58–59.

2 A. Sandauer, '*Rzeczywistość zdegradowana* (Rzecz o Brunonie Schulzu)' [Degraded Reality (About Bruno Schulz)], introduction to *Proza* [Prose] by Bruno Schulz, Wydawnictwo Literackie, Kraków, 1964, pp. 5–43.

3 W. Panas, *Księga blasku. Traktat o kabale w prozie Brunona Schulza* [The Book of Radiance. A Treatise on Kabbalah in Bruno Schulz' Prose], KUL, Lublin 1997.

the creative human personality.[4] Krzysztof Stala has advocated 'a dynamic Schulz,' whose vision of the world and symbolic systems lack stable elements,[5] although even that 'unstable' picture ultimately reveals certain universal regularities, allowing one language to describe all Schulz's stories.

Another aspect of the holistic in Schulz's writing is its wealth of associations and references to mythology, symbolic languages of culture, history, biology, science, psychology, literature, and the like. Schulz makes such references neither to boast of his erudition, nor to quote works by great masters, nor to drop names, but, on the contrary, to camouflage his allusions to mythic and religious understandings of the world. Hence the Old and New Testament, Kabbalah, the myths of ancient Greece and Babylon – all these texts are held up against Schulz's fictions in order to see fragments, mirror shards,[6] reflecting individual elements of mythic stories. Thus the interpreter wanting to comprehend this writer continually labours to reconstruct, to sketch out everything Schulz's writing directly refers or at least alludes to. When Schulz's fiction is furnished with its "missing parts," it appears truly monumental; it seems a vast, universal blueprint for the order of creation, with elements of cosmogony, biology and anthropology equally represented, since human beings cannot be understood without reference to the history of culture, as well as to natural history in its broadest perspective.

Yet it is difficult to deny that the image of the Whole is almost non-existent in Schulz's world. On the contrary, his world is dominated by visions of the fragmentariness of reality in all its incompleteness and minuteness, as well as of the fragmentariness of the text the kind that Kazimierz Bartoszyński calls

---

4 J. Jarzębski, *Czasoprzestrzeń mitu i marzenia w prozie Brunona Schulza. Powieść jako autokreacja* [The Time and Space of Myth and Dream in Bruno Schulz's Prose, Novel as Self-creation] Wydawnictwo Literackie, Kraków, 1984, pp. 170–226; J. Jarzębski, *Schulz,* Wydawnictwo Śląskie, Wrocław 2000; J. Jarzębski, op. cit., 2005.

5 K. Stala, *Na marginesach rzeczywistości. O paradoksach przedstawiania w twórczości Brunona Schulza* [On the Margins of Reality. About the Paradoxes of Represenation in Bruno Schulz's Work], Instytut Badań Literackich, Warszawa, 1995.

6 It is no coincidence that the anniversary volume of the Lublin proceedings is entitled *W ułamkach zwierciadła… Bruno Schulz w 110 rocznicę urodzin i 60 rocznicę śmierci* [In Mirror Shards... Bruno Schulz on the 110th Anniversary of His Birth and the 60th Anniversary of His Death], eds. M. Kitowska-Łysiak and W. Panas, Towarzystwo Naukowe KUL, Lublin, 2003.

'structural'.[7] Thus we could come to regard "the scrap of paper" as Schulz's characteristic motif: the remnants of the Book, with only the last pages saved, filled with advertising announcements that appeal to the reader's base emotions and unofficial yearnings. The universal order then becomes a postulate, a premise,[8] but we actually cannot see it; instead, we co-exist with what Poulet calls indeterminacy, or, to follow Rilke, Schulz's master, 'a free union of indeterminacy and determinacy'.[9] Another of Schulz's masters, Goethe, claims in his *Dichtung und Wahrheit: Aus Meinem Leben* (Poetry and Truth: From My Life):

> One thing is certain, namely, that only the indeterminate (*unbestimmten*), all-embracing emotions of the youth as well as of primitive peoples are capable of understanding the concept of sublimity; that is because the experiencing of sublimity by the souls of individuals or groups is directly connected with the realization, by those individuals or groups, of the fundamentally indeterminate character of this primordial experience.[10]

Schulz's experience, unusually emotional, of 'another childhood' or 'the age of genius', this astonishing eruption of creative imagination typical of the beginnings of a life, clearly has a lot in common with what Goethe describes as the sublime 'dialogue with nature', deprived of intellectual foundations. At the centre of such a return to childhood, Schulz tells us, are certain images that 'constitute a program, establish a cast-iron spiritual investment that we are given very early on as intuitions and half-conscious experiences'. What are

---

7 K. Bartoszyński, *O fragmencie. Powieść w świecie literackości. Szkice* [On the Fragment. The Novel in the World of Literariness. Essays], Instytut Badań Literackich, Warszawa, 1991, p. 149: 'The key to our understanding of structural fragmentariness might be the idea of the openness of suprapredicative structure, e.g. "semantic figure." Hence we could talk about the text being open, if it conditioned such structures that would evade the rules seemingly governing it or attributed to it.'

8 Schulz's protagonist says: 'I knew then that *The Book* is a postulate, that it is a goal'; B. Schulz, *The Book in The Fictions of Bruno Schulz: The Street of Crocodiles and Sanatorium Under the Sign of the Hourglass,* trans. Celina Wieniewska, Picador, London, 1988, p. 129.

9 G. Poulet, *Pensée indeterminée.* The Polish translation, *Myśl nieokreślona,* by T. Swoboda, KR, Warszawa, 2004, p. 275.

10 J.W. Goethe, *Dichtung und Wahrheit*, qtd after Poulet ibid, 2004, p. 180.

these images? They are indeterminate and vaguely symbolic. Schulz recalls the image of 'a child carried by the father across the expanses of vast night and talking to darkness', borrowed from Goethe's *Der Erlkönig (The Alder King)* and expressing its metaphysics.[11] Once again it is a fragment, a piece intended to mirror some whole, but ambiguously, as the individual will never decipher this image completely. Therefore the sense structure is never entirely visible; it always manifests itself through the fragmentary image pointing beyond itself.

In his utterly laconic „Fragment o fragmencie" (*A Fragment about the Fragment*) Walter Hilsbecher proposes that a fragmentary work is the natural outcome of a dream about the unattainable Whole. 'The drive to grasp the whole, which is apparent in [conceptual systems], has its specific function, if only to confirm anew the fragmentary nature of all life phenomena'.[12] We owe this understanding of the function of the fragment to the Romantics, who employed it in order to express the feeling of dissatisfaction, of creative impotence, the inability to attain the whole or to present thought at its birth, at its illumination.[13]

Looking deeper into Schulz's texts, we find that 'fragmentariness' is their main compositional principle. Let us consider language. The idea of the originary Word, of a single protolanguage as the source of all the multifarious linguistic forms we use, presupposes that every word of contemporary language 'is nowadays no more than a fragment, a rudiment of some ancient all-embracing integral mythology'; that it has been incomplete since the very beginnings; that it 'rushes toward thousands of connections',[14] aiming at

---

11 B. Schulz, *Bruno Schulz do St. I. Witkiewicza* [Bruno Schulz to S. I. Witkiewicz], in *Opowiadania. Wybór esejów i listów* [Stories. Selected essays and letters], ed. J. Jarzębski, 2nd. Ed., Zakład Narodowy im. Ossolińskich, Wrocław and Kraków, 1998, pp. 474–475.

12 W. Hilsbecher, *Fragment o fragmencie. Tragizm, absurd i paradoks. Eseje* [A Fragment about the Fragment. Tragedy, Absurdity and Paradox. Essays], sel. and intro. S. Lichański, trans. S. Błaut, Państwowy Instytut Wydawniczy, Warszawa, 1972, p. 153.

13 Those Romantics who used the poetics of the fragment include Shelley, Coleridge, Poe, Macpherson, Byron; in Poland these were Krasiński and Słowacki; Friedrich Schlegel and Novalis formulated their thoughts on the subject (cf. M. Konarzewska, the *Fragment* entry in *Słownik rodzajów i gatunków literackich* [A Dictionary of Literary Genres and Terms], eds. G. Gazda and S. Tynecka-Makowska, Universitas, Kraków, 2006.

14 B. Schulz, *Mityzacja rzeczywistości* [The Mythologization of Reality], in *Opowiadania....* op. cit.,p. 383.

'completing itself into meaning'.[15] This meaning is not some popularly understood 'logical coherence,' but a mythological notion. It therefore points to no particular mythic plot, at the same time remaining in a stable relationship with a series of words that add up to an image or a story. At the level of language we probably could perceive the following regularity most clearly: in Schulz's work one believes in the existence (at the beginning of the world, *in potentia*) of the Whole as the primordial Word-Logos, whereas one must contend with a desacralized mass of words for interpersonal communication.

The memory of this primordial unity is retained in the process of metaphorization, which – in its poetic capacity – brings together words from various realms of reality and thus creates new concepts. The metaphor, that particular place, that spot in the text, where one textual element finds itself incorporated into an unfamiliar context, into a sequence of associations leading towards a different destination than one might expect from the original context. We might therefore conclude that a metaphorized text consists of a number of local word-events that branch out semantically and figuratively into a multi-layered construction. Let us consider a convenient example:

> And while the children's games became increasingly noisier and more complicated, while the city's flushes darkened into purple, the whole world suddenly began to wilt and blacken and exude an uncertain dusk which contaminated everything. Treacherous and poisonous, the plague of dusk spread, passed from one object to another, and everything it touched became black and rotten and scattered into dust. People fled before it in silent panic, but the disease always caught up with them and spread in a dark rash on their foreheads. Their faces disappeared under large, shapeless spots. They continued on their way, now featureless, without eyes, shedding as they walked one mask after another, so that the dusk became filled with the discarded larvae dropped in their flight. Then a black, rotting bark began to cover everything in large putrid scabs of darkness.[16]

---

[15] ibid., p. 384.

[16] B. Schulz, The Night of the Great Season, in *The Fictions of Bruno Schulz...* op. cit., pp. 89 – 90.

The image that arises here is that of dusk passing through the town and reimagined as a universal skin disease: in objects, the disease assumes a vegetative form ('wilting,' 'blackening,' 'rotting,' 'scattering into dust'); in humans it is a leprosy of sorts, causing skin to peel off. Something happens between the words, a local event: as far as I can remember, Schulz does not repeat it anywhere else; this spark is created only here, a leap between these layers of the world structure and lexical meaning rather than any other. Such brief, fragmentary tensions help Schulz erect a sense of the world, that is, a system of meanings and an image of universal processes analogous to those in reality.[17] For Schulz, metaphor is something deeply significant, and its function can be compared to the role it performed in Tadeusz Peiper's avant-garde theory of poetry, although for Peiper it constituted the building material of 'a purely poetic reality', whereas for Schulz it constructed 'a primordial reality', pointing towards the foundation myth of humankind.[18]

Fragmentariness appears also as an idea in 'Treatise on Tailors' Dummies,' and very peculiarly at that. The father says thus:

> 'We are not concerned', he said, 'with long-winded creations, with long-term beings. Our creatures will not be heroes of romances in many volumes. Their roles will be short, concise; their characters – without a background. Sometimes, for one gesture, for one word alone, we shall make the effort to bring them to life. We openly admit: we shall not insist either on durability or solidity of workmanship; our creations will be temporary, to serve for a single occasion. If they be human beings, we shall give them, for example, only one profile, one hand, one leg, the one limb needed for their role. It would be

[17] I discuss the role and functions of Schulz's metaphor in greater detail in my introduction to *B. Schulz* op. cit.: xxxvi-xxxviii as well as in „Zwiedzanie Sklepów cynamonowych" in *Prowincja Centrum. Przypisy do Schulza* [Visiting Cinnamon Shops, Province Centre. Annotating Schulz], Wydawnictwo Literackie, Kraków, 2005, pp. 16–19.

[18] 'Metaphor … is a wilful relation of notions; it is the creating of notional compounds, which do not have equivalents in the real world. Therefore, it is not the means of the realistic imitation of the world. It is not a slavish inventory of reality. It is not a description. Transferring notions into the districts where they do not belong according to the register, metaphor transforms the reality of experiences and turns it into a new reality, a purely poetic reality.' T. Peiper, „Metafora teraźniejszości" in *Tędy: Nowe usta* [Metaphor of The Present, This Way; A New Mouth], Wydawnictwo Literackie, Kraków, 1972, pp. 54–55.

> pedantic to bother about the other, unnecessary, leg. Their backs can be made of canvas or simply whitewashed. We shall have this proud slogan as our aim: a different actor for every gesture. For each action, each word, we shall call to life a different human being. Such is our whim, and the world will be run according to our pleasure.'[19]

The father seems to refer to the avant-garde theory of art, which back then ostentatiously turned its back on realistic illusion-making and favoured cubism or constructivism, the principle of overlaying various elements on the surface, instead of creating the appearance of a three-dimensional, quasi-real space that points beyond itself, pretending to be a fragment of a larger reality. Here it is as if the fragment remains the entire available reality, at the same time as it demonstrates its 'incompleteness,' its ultimate utility within the work of art.

Schulz frequently resorts to this method while constructing his protagonists. He ushers into his stories a gallery of characters who make only a single appearance: Aunt Agatha and her family, Touya and her mother, Maria, Polda and Paulina, the tramp from the story 'Pan,' Uncle Charles, Professor Arendt, the senior shop assistant Theodore, Aunt Perasia, even the small dog Nimrod – to name only the protagonists of *Cinnamon Shops;* in *Sanatorium Under the Sign of the Hourglass* the situation looks similar. These protagonists exist in the stories thanks to one particular, distinct trait of their character or appearance: they do not come with their history, they appear and soon vanish for ever. If we were to look more closely at the protagonists that keep reappearing, their fragmentariness will readily reveal itself. What do we really know about Adela, apart from the fact that she was very orderly, and voluptuous, as well as self-confident? What do we know about the mother, apart from the fact that she was a housekeeper, that she was 'down-to-earth,' that is, indifferent to the father's outbursts of whimsy. And, finally, what about the father himself – that he was a chronically ailing old man, an eccentric merchant gifted with fantasy and creative passion who became even more eccentric with age but always fond of women?

Following these short-lived figures, these characters with no future plans, Schulz's stories can be equally temporary, with no insistence on workmanship and finish, that is, without any 'pre-action' explaining where the characters

[19] B. Schulz, *Treatise on Tailors' Dummies, or The Second Book of Genesis,* in *The Fictions of Bruno Schulz...* op. cit., p. 41.

have come from, and without a concluding point. For this reason Schulz scholars often talk about the description dominating the narrative. Schulz's stories are usually brief, fleeting, deprived of plot development, reduced to a character sketch or a description of some situation ('Mr. Charles', 'Pan', 'Dodo', 'Eddie', 'Nimrod', 'My Father Joins the Fire Brigade', 'Fall', 'A Second Fall', 'Fatherland', 'A Republic of Dreams'). Even the stories with more clearly developed plots have a rather unresolved, seemingly suspended, ending ('Cinnamon Shops', 'The Book', 'The Age of Genius', 'Spring', 'Sanatorium Under the Sign of the Hourglass', 'The Comet'). In the majority of cases this has to do with Schulz's construction of time: the time of the narrative has for its background a different time, which passes independently: this is a mythic, circular time, with a predetermined sequence of phases. Accordingly, 'Spring' must come to nothing for its protagonist, for the story ends with summer, and thus the nature of the world changes, and with it our susceptibility to revolutionary slogans. Similarly in 'Cinnamon Shops', where fantasmagoria must come to an end with daybreak; likewise in 'The Age of Genius', which lasts as long as its protagonist's childhood, and finishes with the discovery of 'the sheaf of paper', which introduces the boy to the perversions of the erotic. 'The Comet' is dangerous as long as the 'fashion' for an astronomical apocalypse lasts. I once wrote that in 'Spring' there occurred a peculiar phenomenon of resonance: the protagonist's youth coincided with the 'youthful' season of the year.[20] That is why we could see right from the start that the spring in the story 'was more real, more dazzling and brighter than any other spring'.[21] When the resonance disappears, however, the story loses its energy and fades away.

Zeew Fleischer, Schulz's ex-student living in Beer Sheva, has told me that the famous 'tales' spun by his drawing teacher during a class lasted as long as the class itself. They ended abruptly the moment the bell rang to announce the break, and Schulz would never come back to them. So what happened resembled Schulz's written fictions: they broke off with the beat of this 'time-metre', whose clock tick-tocked in the background of the story. This background clock was therefore always more powerful than the inner clock of the narrative.

Bruno Schulz's plots are necessarily fragmentary; begun in mythic time, they disregard its structure; they eternally wish to maintain their own

20 Cf. J. Jarzębski, *Wstęp* [Introduction] in B. Schulz, *Opowiadania*... op. cit., pp. LVII–LVIII.

21 B. Schulz, *Spring*, in *The Fictions of Bruno Schulz*... op. cit., p. 150.

diagnosis of the world and the story that matches it. An outside intervention stops this delusion: for Schulz the existence of the world itself is a plot, recurrent and somehow 'circular', and therefore deprived of final resolutions while also providing a model for all other plots. But it is exactly for this reason that this masterplot does not allow the existence and perseverance of those other, rival plots, which tend towards some closure, some triumph of the signifying construction. Schulz allows them to last for a brief moment and to harmonize heroically with his cosmic 'mega-narrative', though as a matter of fact he condemns them to a short life and a sudden end, or they blur into indeterminacy. What remains is the eternal recurrence of mythic time and the universal sequence of events ordered by it.

In Schulz's world, then, each plot resolution is naturally dubious, as it contradicts the order of the world, where everything runs endlessly, to the rhythm of continual renewal. Even death does not end anything: at the conclusion of 'Father's Last Escape' the father-crustacean will crawl on, to the rhythm of the never-ending adventure of renewable life, as he did before when, seemingly absent, he suddenly appeared as a condor or returned in his afterlife in 'Sanatorium Under the Sign of the Hourglass'. However, this absence of death-as-endpoint may be poignant and tragic. Schulz's stories are full of protagonists trapped forever in some form of existence whose sense cannot be detected. As is the case with Touya, Eddie, Dodo, Uncle Jerome. Their forms of existence are not plot-like, as they do not progress toward any destination, any conclusion; they can be described only from outside, with a specific entomological flair. The same fate befalls Uncle Edward, who, as a martyr to science, wishes to sacrifice himself and to be 'physically reduced, for the benefit of science, to the bare principle of Neeff's hammer'.[22] In this way Uncle Edward moves from the dramatic reality of 'the foreground' of his existence to the background, where the impersonal laws of nature are made manifest, resulting as it does for the crippled protagonists in his permanent 'entrapment' in some determinate form of existence. Paradoxically, the fate of a retired pensioner seems to be most conclusive and meaningful: in his old age he simply returns to his childhood, and finally he is carried off by the autumn wind to disappear into thin air, as if he were a wilted leaf and, in this form, returning to nature. Even in the story entitled 'August', which is a glorification of fertility, of passing to offspring the opportunity to realize a meaningful plot in existence, we can find either 'aberrant' reproduction (for

[22] Bruno Schulz, "The Comet" in *The Fictions of Bruno Schulz...* op. cit., p. 104.

example, Touya and her dead mother, Maria) or reproduction ashamed of its own, almost animalistic, explicitness (Aunt Agatha and her daughters) and thus escaping into perversity (Cousin Emil).

The aesthetics of the fragment played a major role in twentieth-century literature and avant-garde art, a subject thoroughly discussed by Maria Delaperrière.[23] Basically, she distinguishes between two functions of the fragment in modern tradition:

> Initially, the fragment is a form of subversion, a protest against the whole, regardless of whether that whole is called unity, Transcendentialism, totalitarianism, or system, and it may express an openly manifested freedom or defeat, nostalgia or creative impotence. Only in the second phase does it become the metonymy of the disintegrated contemporary world. In the first case the fragment is a constructive destruction, a rebellion against classical order in the name of a new order, thus resembling various modernist utopias; in the second case, it results from the end of modernity revealing numerous aporias, which are typically considered under the common heading of postmodernism. In the first case we talk about the fragmentary aesthetics as a protest against all systems, as the undermining of meanings, as polyphony; in the second case, it is the aesthetics of 'disintegration', born out of the melancholic conviction that everything has already been said.[24]

How does it work for Schulz? Delaperrière devotes a mere three sentences to him, though she does claim that he inspired contemporary writers fighting for the integration of their own 'I':

> Schulz took advantage of the fragmentariness of imagination; he fished for scraps of memories, among which were a nostalgia for the return to 'The Great Book' and a new genesis, which much earlier had afflicted Mallarmé. The assembling

23 M. Delaperrière, *Fragment i całość, czyli Dylematy nowoczesności* [The Fragment and the Whole, or Dilemmas of Modernity], *Teksty Drugie, nr.* 3, 1997, pp. 21–42.

24 ibid., pp. 21–22.

> of pieces of one's own mythology and their inclusion in the universal mythology already required the integration of identity, which became all the more urgent after the war.[25]

Perhaps this was what happened; however, it is difficult to overlook the peculiar quality of Schulz's stories, the aforementioned incoherence between the individual narratives, which tend toward some reasonable closure, and the circular 'great plot' of nature or of the cosmos, which has no use for such local meanings, as its significance lies in the continual renewal and the 'eternal now' of myth. Delaperrière also remarks on this:

> the fragment as an emblem of modernity referred to two opposing, though consecutive, modernist notions: that of Hegel and that of Nietzsche. According to Hegel, that which is individual can co-exist with the whole, but under special circumstances, which Hegel called 'being together', namely, in a compromise thanks to which the involved parties, meaningless on their own, start to matter the moment they are included in a set of elements constituting some whole. Nietzsche, on the other hand, considered the fragment an autonomous whole, functional and meaningful regardless of all hierarchies.[26]

At first sight it would be difficult to classify Schulz according to these categories: it is true that in his writing the fragment always exists against the background of the whole and in a very close relationship with it, but, on the other hand, the reconciliation of the two is impossible. What is individual cannot easily fit into the holistic vision of the universe. Hence the role of irony in Schulz's understanding of existence.[27] Let us quote here a frequently cited passage which talks about the rules to which the world of 'Cinnamon Shops' adheres:

> A certain extreme monism of the life is assumed here, for which specific objects are nothing more than masks. The life

25 ibid., p. 41.

26 ibid., pp. 25–26.

27 Cf. Piotr Millati's and Włodzimierz Bolecki's entries on irony in *Słownik schulzowski* [Schulz Dictionary], eds. W. Bolecki, J. Jarzębski and S. Rosiek, Słowo/Obraz/Terytoria, n.d., Gdańsk, 2003. See also J. Jarzębski, *Prowincja Centrum.....*, op. cit., pp. 126–128.

> of the substance consists in the assuming and consuming of numberless masks. This migration of forms is the essence of life. Thus an all-pervading aura of irony emanates from this substance. There is an ever-present atmosphere of the stage, of sets viewed from behind, where the actors, make fun of the pathos of their parts after stripping off their costumes. The bare fact of separate individual existence holds an irony, a hoax, a clowns stuck-out tongue.[28]

This ironic quality of existence can be explained, I think, by the incompatibility of the individual being and the being of the world as a whole. That is why none of the roles adopted by the individual can be permanent; each remains fragmentary, briefly assumed, because ultimately it will conflict with the fundamentally non-dramatic, eternally recurrent, plot of the (mythological) background of the events.

Schulz's reality may be affected by one more category of fragmentariness, that which is connected to one's awareness of a great catastrophe and the debris it leaves in its wake. Maria Delaperrière quotes Blanchot, who

> influenced by growing postmodernist tendencies, defines the fragment as the only island on in the contemporary epoch's sea of ruins ('when everything has been said, what is left to be said is defeat, the ruins of the world, the inefficiency of writing, the static that is the whisper of what is left without remainder').[29]

Schulz's 'ruins' are, obviously, merely a vague premonition of postmodernist exhaustion; they are more readily associated with the ruins left behind by the value crisis at the turn of the twentieth century and by the catastrophe of the Second World War, as intuited by Schulz. Next to the fragmentary vision of individual existence there appears the vision of the whole human culture as a ruin. Consider this characteristic quote from 'Journeys of a Sceptic':

---

[28] B. Schulz, *An Essay for S. I. Witkiewicz*, transl. by Wiesiek Powaga in *The Collected Works of Bruno Schulz*, ed. Jerzy Ficowski, Picador, London, 1998, p. 369.

[29] M. Blanchot, *Écritures du désastre*, Gallimard, Paris, 1980, p. 79; qtd after M. Delaperrière, op.cit., pp. 29.

> The walks of a sceptic through the ruins of culture. Far and wide, rubble and dust. The traveller has found everything in ruins, ploughed along and across by the plow of untiring human thought. The traveller carefully puts his walking-stick to the ground, pauses, resting on it, smiles. Then he digs with his walking-stick melancholically in the rubble: problems and problems, fractions and fragments of problems. Here a broken-off head looks askew, there a leg digs itself out, clambers and limps lonely across the rubbish pit.[30]

This view of culture as ruins is common to numerous twentieth-century artists and thinkers (Adorno, Bataille). Eugenio Donato sees the roots of this phenomenon in earlier epochs, in Romanticism, when it turns out that the human mind cannot make 'the natural object' present here and now, constantly referring us to memory filled with the rubble of the fragments of textual representations.[31]

This type of fragmentariness differs from that which I have already discussed. That earlier fragmentariness was structural and timeless in character; it resulted from the difference between the universal plot realizing itself in circular mythic time and the always fragmentary life-plots of the individuals, directed toward some destination or point. This new fragmentariness is historical and results from the state of culture. This is why Schulz writes about the fragmentariness of the cultural message in an up-to-date review, situated in the present, whereas the other fragmentariness is located in childhood stories. It is difficult to fight against or disagree with the image of culture as ruins; yet Schulz finds in his stories a remedy for such a conviction. If culture falls to pieces, it might be in transition – is it an anticipation of some great change?

Walter Hilsbecher, whom I have already quoted, says: 'Historically speaking, the fragment plays an essential role at the beginning and at the end of all great formal epochs. It introduces them in a sketchy manner or resolves them into constituent materials which can be used for later projects. Between the

---

30 B. Schulz, *Wędrówki sceptyka* [Journeys of a Sceptic] in *Opowiadania...* op.cit., pp. 425–426.

31 E. Donato, 'Ruiny pamięci: Fragmenty archeologiczne i artefakty tekstowe', [The Ruins of Memory: Archeological Fragments and Textual Artifacts], Polish trans. D. Gostyńska, *Pamiętnik Literacki*, nr. 3, Związek Pisarzy Polskich na Obczyźnie, London, 1986, pp. 319–339.

beginning and the end fragmentarists recede into the background'.[32] Indeed, in Schulz's writing, as in Hilsbecher's, the beginning of a new epoch sees the fragmentation of language and the preference for fleeting, ecstatic, emotional forms. Thus Schulz associates spring with a manifesto, a telegram, a horoscope.[33] Unlike summer, with its fantastic grandiloquence, autumn looks for boundaries, it limits shapes to what is concrete ('Autumn is the longing of a human soul for physicality, gravity, boundaries'[34]). The autumnal fragmentation has different origins and forms than the spring one, though its meaning is similar: it stems from the realization that dreams about the Whole, about the Absolute, never come true. In this way the mechanism that earlier had prevented individuals from fulfilling their dream of existence made meaningful through accomplishment now assumes the opposite: by showing the limitations of every dream, it prepares individuals to accept the end in anticipation of the inevitable rebirth. What was initially supposed to take away hope and prospects for the future – the image of the world of meaning in ruins – now changes its message: it becomes a consolation and hope for the future.

---

32 Hilsbecher op. cit., 154.

33 Cf. B. Schulz, *Wiosna* [Spring] in *Opowiadania...* op. cit., p. 143.

34 B. Schulz, *Jesień* [Autumn], *Opowiadania...* op. cit., pp. 337–338.

Veneration and Desecration : The Afterlife of Bruno Schulz

Norman Ravvin – Concordia University

Abstrait

Bruno Schulz, a difficult writer with a tragic life trajectory, has become a motivating model and presence in the work of writers across a wide variety of world literature. This development has made the life of Schulz well known, while the character of his work - including his pictorial art - has not necessarily been served through these writerly representations. The downfall of some of this interest in Schulz is the centrality of his symbolic currency as a paradigmatic Holocaust victim. The tendency to remake Schulz for the purposes of a work's own goals is most notable in Salman Rushdie's The Moor's Last Sigh, where Schulz is refigured as an avatar of globalism and a multicultural ethic. In this paper I will address these remakings of Schulz in order to explore the motives that support them. I will aim, as well, to address how these remakings damage our ability to know Schulz's work, and to what extent they aid us in reading him.

There is a building on Nowy Świat – if you know Warsaw you might recognize it – a three-story grey granite villa with a broad opening into the back courtyard and a black wrought iron balcony attached to its top floor windows. It is at number 33, and there lived the novelist and playwright Zofia Nałkowska. It was to this address, in 1933, that Bruno Schulz traveled with the manuscript of what would become his first published book to offer it up for judgement and hoped-for patronage. In his *Regions of the Great Heresy*, Jerzy Ficowski tells us that Schulz, upon receiving a phone call announcing Nałkowska's very positive response, stood 'as if rooted to the floor, paralyzed'.[1] One can stand across the street from number 33 Nowy Świat and imagine this scene of literary assumption, though the buses grunting by are loud and modern, and the students strolling on the broad sidewalk affect a distinctly Americanized look. Still, one can see Schulz arrive in a taxi, his manuscript in a briefcase, in order for the patroness to transform his future. The contemporary street scene does not preclude the possibility – if one is inclined to indulge – of veneration.

[1] J. Ficowski, *Regions of the Great Heresy: A Biographical Portrait.* trans. T. Robertson. Norton, New York, 2003.

Desecration presents itself as a more common theme in the postwar representation of Schulz – and I refer here to the context of Schulz's rise to the status of icon among writers and critics. He has attained an importance acquired by only a few of the celebrated twentieth-century modernists – Henry James, James Joyce, and Franz Kafka are among those who come to mind – writers who, for other writers, have become touchstones for their art, talismanic and necessary figures who supply inspiration and are in turn transformed into literary material. One thinks of this as an act of veneration, as the acolyte acclaims, through his devotion, a saintly genius. But the outcome in the case of Schulz is something stranger and darker, a kind of ongoing act of desecration through creative transformation.

The best-known triumvirate of venerators – unfairly, I'll argue, lumped together – are the Israeli writer David Grossman, the U.S. novelist Cynthia Ozick and Philip Roth.[2] David Goldfarb calls *See Under: Love, The Messiah of Stockholm* and *The Prague Orgy* 'Schulz-derivative literature', distinguishing them from the work of such figures as Danilo Kiš and Tadeusz Kantor, who, Goldfarb tells us, incorporate 'Schulz's figures and icons into their own creation, rather than dwelling on the trope of Bruno Schulz, the man'.[3] Ozick and Grossman, Goldfarb explains, introduce Schulz as 'a fictionalized character or lost literary father'. Kantor and Kiš, on the other hand, can be said to 'claim without irony the entire interwar Polish avant-garde as part of their living literary heritage and should be seen as the legitimate bearers of that aesthetic into the postwar age'. Goldfarb, in a more sophisticated manner than is often the case, raises the question of where Schulz's life and work can best be said to belong: in the Polish milieu; as part of a community of interwar avant-gardists; in a Jewish context; and so on. In Goldfarb's view, the venerators bring to their 'Schulz-derivative work' their own fatal point of view – that is, their limited understanding of eastern Europe as 'quite literally a dead world'. For them – and here he rightly singles out Ozick – the lack of comprehension and sympathy for prewar cultural life creates an inevitable aridity, a superficial invocation of Schulz as man and writer, lacking in any appreciation of the context in which he lived and worked. Kiš

2 D. Grossman, *See Under: Love.* Washington Square Press, New York , 1989; Cynthia Ozick, *The Messiah of Stockholm,* Vintage, New York, 1987; Philip Roth, *The Prague Orgy. Zuckerman Bound: A Trilogy and Epilogue.* Fawcett, NewYork, 1985, p. 423–72.

3 D. Goldfarb, *A Living Schulz: Noc wielkiego sezonu* (The Night of the Great Season). http://www.echonyc.com/~goldfarb/schulz.htm

and Kantor, Goldfarb might say, are properly Schulzian, while the others are merely Schulz-obsessed.

A recent and characteristically acute essay by Milan Kundera, entitled *Die Weltliteratur,* helps us further refine our sense of this predicament. Kundera explores the way a writer can be read in what he calls 'the small context', within the history of his national culture, as well as in 'the large context' that is part of a 'supranational history' or 'Weltliteratur'.[4] Kundera points to how differently French literature is read at home and away, and even more sharply, he accounts for the manner in which his own work, and that of Kafka before him, is viewed from the point of view of French readers. Kundera points to a tendency among readerly communities to fashion a symbolic frame within which to read an author. This frame can have little or nothing at all to do with a text's specific historical, linguistic or social particularities. Rather, through this frame a writer is transformed, by way of peculiar strategies of interpretation, into something quite unlike himself, the outcome being a kind of literary vampire, a revenant version that dines for the foreseeable future upon the original. Of his own experience of this, Kundera reflects on the uniformity with which he has been read as a literary voice from the 'Slavic world', a novelist descending from Dostoyevsky, Gogol and Pasternak. 'I admire them all', Kundera says of the Russians, 'but in their company I became a different person'.

Notable in the work of the venerators – or, if we follow Goldfarb's line, the Schulz-derivative writers – is the graphic repetition of the details of his murder. In this, Schulz's life is viewed, one might say, through the wrong end of the telescope. Numerous critics – including even Jerzy Ficowski in his introduction to the Penguin paperback edition of *The Street of Crocodiles* – start here as well. Ficowski begins:

> On November 19, 1942, in the streets of Drohobycz, a small provincial town that belonged to Poland before World War II ... there commenced a so called action...[5]

In the same edition the translator's preface reiterates these details, as of course do the back cover biographical notes. In *The Messiah of Stockholm* Ozick

[4] M. Kundera, *Die Weltliteratur,* The New Yorker, Jan. 8, 2007. pp. 28–35.

[5] J. Ficowski, *Introduction* in B. Schulz, *The Street of Crocodiles,* Penguin, New York, 1977, pp. 13–22.

presents Schulz's murder as a point of fascination for a key character, though this theme is not developed:

> It was the shooting that drew her. The shooting; the murder. Shot in the streets! ... it was the catastrophe of fact she wanted, Lars's father gunned down in the gutters of Drohobycz along with two hundred and thirty other Jews. A Thursday in 1942... Lars's father was bringing home a loaf of bread.

David Grossman's approach to this material has a different aim, but the details are reiterated all the same. Grossman writes, as if to begin a biographical entry:

> Bruno Schulz. A Jew. Possibly the most important Polish writer between the two world wars. Son of the eccentric owner of a dry-goods store. Taught drawing and technical drafting at the Drohobycz Gymnasium. A lonely man.
>
> And in 1941, when the Germans entered the city of Drohobycz, Bruno was forced to leave his home and move to a house on Stolarska Street. Under orders from the authorities, he painted giant murals at the riding academy and catalogued libraries commandeered by the Germans. To earn a living, he also worked as a 'House Jew' (light carpentry, sign painting, family portraits, etc.) at the residence of the SS Officer Felix Landau.
>
> Felix Landau had an enemy – another SS officer by the name of Karl Gunther. On November 19, 1942, on the corner of Czackiego and Mickiewicz Streets, Karl Gunther shot Bruno and, as the story goes, went to Landau and said, 'I killed your Jew.' To which Landau replied, 'In that case, I will now kill your Jew.'

Grossman repeats the details of this event in reverse order to other sources, in rather inelegant prose, making awkward use of transliterations from the Polish. Still, this scenario recurs in *See Under: Love* in support of the narrator's assertion that such acts are what his book means to write against. In a talk given as part of a symposium in 2001, entitled *The Future of the Holocaust: Story-telling, Memory, Identity,* Grossman recounts an anecdote in support of this commitment.[6] It was a friend in Israel, whom he calls a 'new immigrant from Poland', who directed him to Schulz. Grossman then 'read the whole book' – he is apparently referring to *Cinnamon Shops* – 'without knowing anything about its writer'. In the editor's epilogue to *Cinnamon Shops* Grossman encountered what he calls 'the story of the death of Schulz'. He recounts it for his audience in a slightly different form than its appearance in *See Under: Love,* with an accent on the taunts of 'your Jew / my Jew'. 'I didn't want to live', Grossman explained to his audience, 'in a world where such a language can exist and allow such monstrous events to take place . . .'

Whereas Ozick presents Schulz's murder as a site of fascination, and Grossman raises it – both in his fiction and in public pronouncements – as a site of moral instruction, Philip Roth is cannier in his use of the factual details in *The Prague Orgy.* Here, Roth's perennial alter ego, Nathan Zuckerman, is approached by a stranger named Zdenek Sisovsky, who tells the story of his European inheritance, which includes a description of his father's writing life and violent death. In most of its details, this description mirrors those connected with Schulz. Against his own better instincts, Zuckerman finds himself in Prague, where he convinces Zdenek's ex-wife to show him the elder Sisovsky's literary oeuvre. Roth, too, represents the 'He shot my Jew, so I shot his' scenario, but the occasion of its telling in Zuckerman's Manhattan apartment creates something more concrete and instructive than its application by Ozick or Grossman. Zuckerman must contend with a European past that is alien and challenges his own Jewish American identity. In Prague, where he manages to see the stories that are meant to be those of Zdenek's murdered father, the impact on Zuckerman is abrupt, tactile and in certain ways transformative:

> *I untie the ribbon on the box. Inside, hundreds of pages of unusually thick paper, rather like the heavy waxed paper that oily foodstuffs used to be wrapped in at the grocery. The ink is black, the margins perfect, the Yiddish script is sharp and neat. None of the stories seems longer than five or six pages. I can't read them.* (emphasis Roth's)

[6] D. Grossman, *Holocaust, Storytelling, Memory, Identity: David Grossman in California,* Feb. 25. 2001. Http://findarticles.com/p/articles/mi_m0411/is_1/51/ai_85068470

Here the focus of Roth's narrative veers away from Schulz himself, from the details of his death, and certainly away from his two influential volumes of prose, since what Zuckerman tracks down is *someone else's* stories. One might argue that in *The Prague Orgy* the historical Schulz is used as a diversion, a decoy, by which Roth leads his alter ego and his reader toward uniquely new challenges: the meaning of prewar Europe for postmodern American Jewish writing; the ghostly presence of Yiddish as the language in which that world's daily life and much of its literary economy were inscribed; the possibility that after evading all concern with these things one might be forced to rethink one's relationship with the past. There is no symbolic Schulz in *The Prague Orgy*. Rather, there is a return to history, to particularity and to self-knowledge. This strategy, one might argue, is a fictive counterpart to the editorial approach taken by Roth in his *Writers from the Other Europe* series, where communicating the literary and historical context of the works being translated for western readers was a paramount feature of the editor's goals.

Contrary to this, the impetus in both *See Under: Love and The Messiah of Stockholm* is the creation of a symbolic or mythic version of Schulz. As Goldfarb suggests, Ozick and Grossman invoke his 'figure as a trope in their own stories' and incorporate 'a fictionalized character or lost literary father based on the actual Schulz'. '[F]or me, Bruno is the key', Grossman's narrator tells us. He is 'an invitation and a warning'. And then the narrator, who is in the process of devising a book about the aftermath of the Holocaust, adds the following:

> Now I write with a steady pen: Bruno Schulz. Ingenious architect of a singular linguistic experience, the magic of which lies in its fertility, a plethora almost rotting with verbal juices. Bruno who knows how to say everything in ten different ways, each as accurate as the compass needle. A Don Juan of language, conquering with a mad, almost immoral passion, audacious explorer of linguistic geography . . . Could it be that you, Bruno, reached the limits of this world, and ran around like a madman on the beach when you couldn't find a suitable verbal vessel to sail . . . did you laugh triumphantly and with relief for having led us all astray through your intricate labyrinths, slyly destroying the very language of humanity?

Such mythifying could only occur in fiction: the critics and reviewers are barred from such flourishes and curlicues.

Ozick, in *The Messiah of Stockholm,* quotes from Schulz's work, and names a key character in her narrative after Schulz's Adela, the dominating house servant of Cinnamon Shops. In a direct borrowing, Ozick makes use of italics as the only sign that her novel uses Schulz's language to describe her character: *'Adela, warm from sleep and with unkempt hair, was grinding coffee in a mill which she pressed to her white bosom, imparting her warmth to the broken beans.'* Ozick's most unnerving borrowing is the use of a Schulz self-portrait for her novel's frontispiece. The Random House paperback includes no acknowledgment of the drawing's ownership, its artifactual character or its relationship to the artistic oeuvre of Schulz. Aside from this image, what is found between the covers of Ozick's novel has nothing to do with the historical Schulz, with the kind of writing he pursued or the culture from which he arose. (Daniel Schwarz, in *Imagining the Holocaust*[7], informs us that after Ozick reviewed *The Street of Crocodiles* Roth sent her two of Schulz's drawings, of which the frontispiece may be one). The drawing is presented at the beginning of Ozick's novel as a calling card, a certificate of the necessary credentials to inscribe Schulz in her fiction. Ultimately, it is an adornment, a bit of grim bric-a-brac to lend *The Messiah of Stockholm* the aura of high European seriousness.

What should we make of the persistent reinscription of Schulz's death in contemporary fiction and criticism? Schulz's iconicity – whether in Ozick's version of a literary mystery, or Grossman's post-Holocaust fantasia – arises largely from the grisly quality of that death, its status as a paradigmatic act of German violence against Jews in occupied eastern Europe. Employed this way, Schulz takes the position in post-Holocaust writing as the anti-Anne Frank. His face becomes emblematic of the Holocaust – this, arguably, is why his self-portrait appears at the start of Ozick's novel – as is Anne's. Hers is associated with youthful idealism and energy. The appearance of her face, a few years ago, as part of a Microsoft ad campaign, suggested that in spite of her death at Bergen-Belsen, she had attained the status of a safe and universal symbol of achievement and high-spirited principles. This must, at least, have been the assumption of the advertising director who thought an association with Anne Frank would ensure software sales. Schulz's afterlife is the inverse of Anne's. He is transmuted into a symbol of the SS proclivity for 'wild actions', the ultimate

7 D. R. Schwarz, *Imagining the Holocaust,* St. Martin's, New York, 1999.

case of a wrong-place-wrong-time fate so common to victims during the war. Anne Frank, on the other hand, has been transformed into the shining young saint of the Holocaust, the image of childish vigour in the face of terrible events, which offers a kind of guarantee of the reappearance of normality in the aftermath of the Holocaust. As a counter-symbol to this, Schulz must go down, again and again, to the murderer's bullet on the Drohobycz street. In critical account after critical account, on book jacket after book jacket, in the prose of would-be acolytes, he is made to become his murder, his life reduced to the wartime German taste for wild public massacres.

It may be revealing to offer one analogy by which to characterize the fate of such an afterlife. Among the iconic images of the Holocaust, recreated on book jackets, on museum gallery walls, as well as in documentary and dramatic film, is a still taken from Soviet newsreel footage shot after the liberation of Auschwitz. A group of children wearing the striped uniforms of camp inmates, with kerchiefs tied about their heads, stands beside the electrified fence under the watchful eyes of Soviet nurses. Among the children's faces is that of a plump five-year-old – the father of a friend of mine. I know the five-year-old's trajectory, his reengagement with postwar life, his successful Canadian adulthood. But to the consumer of Holocaust images, his is the face of Auschwitz. The photograph, and so, too, his childhood self, have become both public property and part of the material with which publishers and editors make the Holocaust knowable. My friend's father then has two faces: his own changing visage, and another, unchanging, which has become symbolic of Auschwitz. The man met his own symbolic face on a movie screen in 1970's Calgary, when watching *The Nuremberg Trials.* Soviet footage of Auschwitz appeared on the screen, and he said aloud, 'Hey! That's me!'

Though writers have had impressive success with Schulz-centred books, heightening popular awareness of him internationally, I would argue that the outcome of this creative attention – if intended as veneration – is largely negative. Ozick's novel, which garnered widespread critical approbation, is the most embarrassing example of this. But Grossman's big, extravagantly written novel is troubling in its own way, in its tendency toward mythopoeia and abstraction. Judging by the book's reviews, the great majority of its readers are surprisingly untroubled to discover Schulz imagined as an escapee from the Drohobycz ghetto, about to leap into the waters at the port of Gdańsk, where he will turn, magical-realistically, into an underwater creature.

Two further books, at opposite poles of the growing catalogue of Schulz-inspired literature, are worthy of consideration. The first of these is Salman

Rushdie's *The Moor's Last Sigh*[8], his first novel to follow *The Satanic Verses. The Moor's Last Sigh* is primarily a novel of Indian politics, as well as a family portrait of its main character, who is nicknamed the Moor. The novel's setting shifts, toward its end, to Andalusia, where the legacy of southern Spain's fate under Arab and Catholic rule becomes an additional context within which Rushdie examines contemporary postcolonial identity. In the Andalusian town of Benengeli, what might be dubbed the postcolonial moment is summed up this way:

> I made my way down the little lane and found myself in a most un-Spanish thoroughfare, a "pedestrianised" street full of non-Spaniards – the majority being somewhat elderly, though immaculately turned-out, and the minority young and calculatedly scruffy in the manner of the fashion-conscious classes... This thoroughfare, which, as I would discover, was known by the locals as the Street of Parasites, was flanked by a large number of expensive boutiques – Gucci, Hermès, Aquascutum, Cardin, Paloma Picasso.

As he acquaints himself with the place, the Moor describes feeling as though he

> were in some sort of interregnum, in some timeless zone under the sign of an hourglass in which the sand stood motionless, or a clepsydra whose quicksilver had ceased to flow. . . . I wandered down sausage-festooned streets of bakeries and cinnamon shops . . . . As my Spanish improved, I strayed even further from the Street of Parasites.

For those familiar with Schulzian motifs – or only the titles of his books – these passages allude in obvious ways to key aspects of his work. The stories in *Cinnamon Shops*[9] take place around a precinct of 'doubtful character' called the Street of Crocodiles, which is described as follows:

It was an industrial and commercial district, its soberly utilitarian character glaringly underlined. The spirit of the times, the mechanism of economics, had not spared our city and had taken root in a sector of its periphery which then developed in a parasitical quarter.

[8] S. Rushdie, *The Moor's Last Sigh,* Knopf, Toronto, 1995.

[9] B. Schulz, *The Street of Crocodiles,* trans. C. Wieniewska, Penguin, New York, 1977.

> . . . The pseudo-Americanism, grafted on the old, crumbling core of the city, shot up here in rich but empty and colorless vegetation of pretentious vulgarity. One could see there cheap jerry-built houses with grotesque facades, covered with a monstrous stucco of cracked plaster. . . . Dull, dirty, and faulty glass panes in which dark pictures of the street were wavily reflected, the badly planed wood of the doors, the gray atmosphere of those sterile interiors where the high shelves were cracked and the crumbling walls were covered with cobwebs and thick dust, gave these shops the stigma of some wild Klondike. In row upon row there spread tailors' shops, general outfitters, china stores, drugstores and barbers' saloons. Their large gray display windows bore slanting semicircular inscriptions in thick gilt letters: CONFISERIE, MANUCURE, KING OF ENGLAND.

Rushdie's strategy is not Schulzian in the truest sense, as this is represented in the work of Kiš and Kantor. Nor is it symbolic in the crudest sense, as we have seen in *The Messiah of Stockholm*. Schulz's presence in *The Moor's Last Sigh* is coded, secretive; Schulz is not invoked 'as a trope' in order to enhance a literary legend or myth. Something more idiosyncratic is at work here. Even the Holocaust has been cast aside as the inevitable context within which to view Schulz and his work. We can only guess: was it Schulz's incarceration in a ghetto that leant him an apparent kinship for the fatwa-hounded Rushdie? Was it Rushdie's recognition of his predecessor as a proto-magic realist that drew him to the sweetness of Cinnamon Shops? Or was it the particularities of Drohobycz, in the midst of an oil boom and its transformation from an outpost in a crumbling empire into a kind of Klondike city of hucksters, which seemed analogous to the postcolonial moment Rushdie is prone to burlesquing in his own novels? It would be unfair, I think, to lump this under the rubric of 'Schulz-derivative literature'. Like Roth's novella, *The Moor's Last Sigh* discovers in Schulz's work a frame through which to examine the contemporary scene. And in this, neither Schulz's life nor his work is reduced to symbolic or degraded status. The focus is on the writing, which remains provocative, relevant, a lever for creative unmasking and surprise.

Lastly, let me say a few words about the title piece in Henryk Grynberg's strange and exhilarating collection, called in English *Drohobycz, Drohobycz*

> To podobieństwo, ten pozór, ta nazwa uspokaja nas i nie pozwala nam pytać, kim jest dla siebie ten twór nieszczęśliwy.[25]

> But the resemblance, the pretence, the name reassures us and stops us from asking what that unfortunate figure is in itself and by itself.[26]

In a similar vain, the panopticon is called by the Schulzian narrator 'the great theater of illusion'. The mannequin, on the other hand, which explicitly foregrounds its artificial and illusive character, is defined by Schönle as 'a sign only partially oriented towards its signified'. As such, Jacob's theory can be seen as a subtle critique of those artists who – by taking up a God-like perspective – pretend to recreate reality in a seemingly unproblematic way. They may be said – as Jacob claims with regards to the Demiurge – to try to 'make matter invisible, make it disappear under the surface of life'. Jacob, on the other hand, exclaims:

> Więcej skromności w zamierzeniach, więcej wstrzemięźliwości w pretensjach – panowie demiurdzy – a świat byłby doskonalszy![27]

> More modesty in aspirations, more sobriety in claims, Gentlemen Demiurges, and the world would be more perfect.[28]

Concluding remarks

To conclude, some more attention has to be paid to the obvious poetological connotations of the "Manekiny" cycle. Although the artistic implications of Jacob's discourse have already received considerable critical attention, some remarks directly related to the issue of idolatry should be added. Interestingly, the heretic theory formulated by Jacob does not gain any particular interest among the people who surround him. The Schulzian narrator, Jacob's son,

25 B. Schulz, 1989, op. cit., p. 39.
26 B. Schulz, 1998, op. cit., p. 34.
27 B. Schulz, 1989, op. cit., p. 31.
28 B. Schulz, 1998, op. cit., p. 29.

claims to keep a distance from his father's heretic theories and seems to defy any kind of demiurgic activity. This intention, however, seems to be in opposition to the way the Schulzian narrator himself observes and depicts the surrounding world. The characters from Schulz's stories are very often described 'in the image and likeness' of the mannequin and make their appearance in the form of puppets, automatons, and cardboard figures. This device applies not in the least to the figures that are described in the "Manekiny" cycle itself. At a certain point, the narrator refers to the sewing girls Polda and Paulina in the following way:

> Dziewczęta siedziały nieruchomo z szklanymi oczyma. Twarze ich były wyciągnięte i zgłupiałe zasłuchaniem, policzki podmalowane wypiekami, trudno było w tej chwili ocenić, czy należą do pierwszej, czy do drugiej generacji stworzenia.[29]

> The girls sat motionless, with glazed eyes. Their faces were long and stultified by listening, their cheeks flushed, and it would have been difficult to decide at that moment whether they belonged to the first or the second Genesis of Creation.[30]

Interestingly, this commentary sheds another light on the idol scene in which the girls appear in "Manekiny". Rereading the fragment from a metafictional perspective, the girls may be said to pay tribute not to an ordinary idol, but to the very God in whose image and likeness they have been created, viz. the mannequin from Jacob's theory of second creation. Simultaneously, the sudden immobilization, or automatization, of the sewing girls reveals to the reader that the level of reality on which they appear is nothing but artificial and fictional. More indirectly, this also implies that Jacob, the person with whom they interact and who claims he wishes to create 'in the image and likeness' of the tailors' dummy, turns out to be a creation 'in the image and likeness' of the tailors' dummy himself. The artist himself is being unveiled as an artifact, viz. the product of some secondary creation. As it turns out,

29 B. Schulz, 1989, op. cit., p. 36.

30 B. Schulz, 1998, op. cit., p. 32.

mannequinization is a constitutive and indispensable part of human creativity as such.[31] The aforementioned schedule of first and second creation should be therefore adapted as follows:

	Creation	*Creation*	*Model*
Genesis	God	man	God
Second Creation	mannequin	mannequin	mannequin

This ironic strategy of merging different levels of representation and spreading metafictional confusion seems to be in line with the way Schulz deals with the idea of idolatry in *Xięga Bałwochwalcza.* On the one hand, Schulz in his quality of a creating artist might be said to be outside of the idolatrous paradigm, critically labelling the contents of his book of engravings idolatrous, dealing with the inferior realm of the visual and the sexual. On the other hand, however, by making himself part of the depicted scenes, Schulz seems to side with the idolaters and situates himself within the idolatrous paradigm in an utmost literal way, becoming part of the world of the artifact and the simulacrum. It are these kinds of ironic and auto-ironic gestures that make the 'real Schulz' ever more ungraspable.

[31] It seems to be significant that Schulz uses the plural form of 'manekin' in the title of his short story, although we encounter – strictly speaking – only one tailors' dummy. As the continuation of the "Manekiny" cycle indicates, the human characters turn out to be no less 'mannequinesque' than the tailors' dummy itself.

Pałuby in Bruno Schulz's Workshop

David A. Goldfarb – Barnard College, Columbia University

Abstract

The word 'pałuba' figures prominently in Schulz's Traktat o manekinach. The waxwork figures that Schulz mentions are pałub of a very interesting sort. They are cast from underlying stories. Schulz writes, 'Demiurge, that great master and artist, made matter invisible, made it disappear under the surface of life. We, on the contrary, love its creaking, its resistance, its [pałubiasta] clumsiness' - again the elusive hag, here as an adjective, is lost in translation. A few pages later, the author of the treatise asks, 'Can you imagine the pain, the dull imprisoned suffering, hewn into the matter of that dummy (pałuba) which does not know why it must be what it is, why it must remain in that forcibly imposed form which is no more than a parody?' This is not the 'dummy' (manekin, mannequin) of the title, but a powerful effigy, commensurate with the inchoate power of matter imprisoned in form.

Among the interwar Polish avant-garde, the central question is that of 'form', and this paper considers the concept of pałuba as an element in a Schulzian theory of form. The term, pałuba, enters the language of Polish modernism as the title of a radically experimental novel by the critic and essayist, Karol Irzykowski, and it could be argued that this novel served to liberate writers like Witkacy, Gombrowicz and Schulz in their experiments in prose. Schulz's contribution to this debate might be the notion that there is nothing that does not partake of sublimity when viewed through the 'poetic' imagination capable of identifying and reassembling the lost mythologies in any degraded scrap of matter, revealing the spectrality of its pałubiastość.

Pałuba is a word that confounds all of Schulz's translators and perhaps even native Polish speakers. Jerzy Jarzębski has said that *pałuba* is a Polish word that needs to be translated into Polish every time it is used.[1] Celina Wieniewska cannot settle on a single English word for it in her translation of Schulz, using in one instance 'effigy' and in another case 'dummy', but usually she simply passes it over.[2] She is not alone in this difficulty. One of

[1] Prof. Jarzębski said this in an oral response to an earlier version of this paper in Montreal at the conference entitled *Bruno Schulz: New Readings, New Meanings*, May 4–5, 2007.

[2] B. Schulz, *The complete fiction of Bruno Schulz*, tr. C. Wieniewska, Walker & Co., New York, 1989.

Schulz's French translators, Georges Sidre, renders it alternately as *idole* and *mannequin.*[3] *Mannequin* or 'dummy' risks conflation with the tailor's mannequins or dummies of Schulz's *Traktat o manekinach* (Treatise on Tailor's Dummies) in Wieniewska's version, and while *idole* captures some of the sense of mystery around the word *pałuba* and hints at Schulz's fascination with idolatry in his stories, in his drawings on masochistic religious themes and, above all, in *The Booke of Idolatry* (Xięga bałwochwalcza). *Idole* does not convey the rough-hewn ugliness suggested by *pałuba.* Joseph Hahn renders it consistently, if innocuously, in German as 'der Puppe' (puppet).[4] The German translator's consistency acknowledges the status of pałuba as a keyword (in Raymond Williams' sense) for Schulz, and 'Puppe' is a very interesting choice, since puppets as they are used in the theatre can produce a feeling of the uncanny, but while Schulz's pałuby might be seen as puppets, most puppets could not be seen as *pałuby.* Colleen Taylor Sen, in one of few articles in English[5] on Karol Irzykowski's radically experimental novel entitled *Pałuba* (1903)[6], discusses the word extensively without translating it, acknowledging its resistance to translation in her first footnote.

In the relevant sense for Irzykowski and Schulz, *pałuba* might be translated as 'hag', and it would usually refer to an effigy or doll in the form of a hag. In section two of *August,* for instance, Schulz describes a garden

> there, those protuberant [pałuby of] bur clumps spread themselves like resting peasant women, half-enveloped in their own swirling skirts[7]

The image suggested here (omitted by Wieniewska) is of a roughly carved folk doll, perhaps like a wooden 'świątek' or the straw-stuffed effigy of Marzanna, burned and drowned in an annual festival celebrating the end of winter and the arrival of spring. The assonance of this line

3 B. Schulz, *Les Boutiques de Cannelle,* tr. G. Sidre, T. Douchy, G. Lisowski, Denoël, Paris, 1974, pp. 82–84.

4 B. Schulz, *Die Zimtläden,* tr. Josef Hahn, Carl Hanser Verlag, Munich, 1961, pp. 51–52.

5 C. T. Sen, *Karol Irzykowski's* Pałuba: *A Guidebook to the Future,* SEEJ. 17, Autumn 1973, pp. 288–300.

6 K. Irzykowski, *Pałuba, sny Marii Dunin,* ed. A. Budrecka. Biblioteka Narodowa Ossolineum, Wrocław, 1981.

7 B. Schulz in *Opowiadania, wybór esejów i listów,* ed. J. Jarzębski, Biblioteka Narodowa Ossolineum, Wrocław, 1990, p. 7.

tam te wyłupiaste pałuby łopuchów wybałuszyły się

which Wieniewska hints at in her English version, suggests that perhaps Schulz found a particular poetic quality even in the sound of this word.

The critic and essayist Karol Irzykowski brings the word *pałuba* into the discourse of Polish modernism with his novel, which begins with a dream sequence, followed by a psychoanalytic biography of the main character, and then layers of notes and pseudo-scholarship amending, correcting and negating the previous text. Irzykowski was not otherwise known for fiction, though he was a prolific critic and one of the first European critics to write about cinema in a serious way. While his novel is virtually unknown outside of Poland, it was the break with historical and psychological realism that would free writers like Witkacy, Witold Gombrowicz and Schulz to invent new forms of prose fiction. Schulz in fact mentions Irzykowski's novel in a review of Gombrowicz's novel, *Ferdydurke,* proposing that *Pałuba* was the true predecessor to *Ferdydurke,* but had failed because it was ahead of its time.[8]

Irzykowski is pointedly unclear about the meaning of his title. The authorial persona in the text asserts that it was chosen for its symbolic value, which he only begins to explicate toward the end of the text.[9] It enters the narrative mysteriously as an appellation that Pawełek, the son of the main character, Piotr Strumieński, applies to his deceased mother, Angelika Kauffman. Pawełek is later seduced by the village idiot, known as Kseńka Pałuba. Given that the most relevant meaning of *pałuba* for Irzykowski is a doll in the form of an ugly hag (*pałuba* can also refer to a covered wagon or various other kinds of covering - more on this later), perhaps the title might be taken as a reaction to the *sine qua non* of the nineteenth-century Polish realist novel, another famous 'doll', Bolesław Prus's *Lalka* (The Doll). *Lalka* exemplifies all the characteristics of the genre - a wealthy merchant of the rising middle class in love with a young lady of the declining aristocracy, rich descriptions of material reality, lengthy internal monologues, the background of world politics, the tension between the country and the city, the margins of Europe and the center (i.e., Paris). Irzykowski's *Pałuba* relies on a thin plot - Angelika dies; Strumieński is remarried to a cousin, Ola; Strumieński spends the rest of his life longing for Angelika - relatively little dialogue or direct reporting of characters' thoughts and vague descriptions of places and material culture. Irzykowski regards all

8 K. Irzykowski, op. cit.

9 ibid., pp. 390-391.

these narratives typical of realist fiction as 'little cloaks' (płaszczyki) - conventions of social life that stand in the way of authenticity. Irzykowski's ardently modernist stance toward realism is much like the disdain for Sentimentalism among realists like Dostoevsky and Tolstoy. Irzykowski buries plot beneath piles of metafiction and interventions of the authorial voice.

Irzykowski raises the word *pałuba* to the status of philosophy in the phrase *pierwiastek pałubyczny* - the 'pałubic element'. In the last section of the work, Irzykowski offers something of an explanation, acknowledging that he has self-consciously used an obscure term, rather than something more obvious like 'rectifying element' as a defamiliarizing gesture. Note that *Pałuba* was published fourteen years before Shklovskij would theorize *ostranienie* ('estrangement' or 'defamiliarization') as a literary device in *Art as Technique.* Irzykowski writes

> That which is unlike anything else, should take a name which is unlike anything else, wild and strange, uncombed and unpleasant - uncomfortable to use, and therefore unlikely to become a worn coin.[10]

He wants a word that is unsettling in its own language, let alone in translation.

Sienkiewicz, for instance, uses the word in a brief internal monologue in his novel *The Połaniecki Family* (Rodzina Połanieckich), as a colorful expression that conveys the bluster and naïveté of the character who speaks it to himself. Thinking disdainfully of Aneta's attraction to a 'cherub with the mind of an idiot' by the name of Kopowski, Zawiłowski - a character who admittedly only understands women insofar as he has read about them in books - muses

> A poodle knows better what to say to him. [...] And a woman with such aspirations to understanding, to knowledge, to artistry, to understanding all the shades of thought and feeling could lower herself for such a pałuba. This he did not know how to interpret, even with what he had read about women.[11]

10 ibid., p. 391.

11 H. Sienkiewicz, *Rodzina Połanieckich*, vol. III, *Dzieła*, vol 34, PIW, Warsaw, 1949, p. 32.

What better word to invoke in describing an uninterpretable behavior but a seemingly uninterpretable word. Now interestingly, *pałuba* refers here to the male character - perhaps we would translate it as 'hulk' rather than 'hag' suggesting a lumbering empty shell of a man, recalling the meaning of the word that refers to a covered wagon, which would be the oldest definition, with a citation dating to 1394 in Stanisław Urbańczyk's *Słownik staropolski*. Linde's dictionary also gives the possibility of the masculine pałub as the stump of a tree. In Karłowicz's dictionary, the character Zawiłowski's usage of *pałuba* as a stupid person (głupiec) is the last of eleven definitions and it would correspond nicely to the common English metaphor 'dumb as a stump'.

Irzykowski writes:

> 'Pałuba' is the symbol of everything that shatters the imaginary boundary of a situation from the outside or from the inside, in brutal and dangerous or shameful and shaming form, everything in man that is doubt and uncertainty, pangs of conscience and feelings of incongruity, sin against the Holy Spirit and at the same time His voice, a sentence from the prison tower of egoism to the monstrous precipice of sincerity, the cutting of a nerve that feels only itself and coming to feel the nerve of the world. It is a symbol of the moment in which the ground of what is best and most valued in life is consciously pulled out from under one's feet, the moment of the greatest tribulation and the greatest concentration, the moment of a sudden broadening of the horizon in all directions, the moment of enchantment as the source of a new age, the moment of hyperemotion and hyperoriginality.[12]

As Czesław Miłosz interprets this passage,

> [t]he word *pałuba* (roughly 'hag') [...] stands for all those moments when [...], for a short instant, authenticity penetrates a basic inauthenticity.[13]

---

12 K. Irzykowski, op.cit., p. 391.

13 C. Miłosz, *The History of Polish Literature*, 2nd edn., University of California Press, Berkeley, 1983, p. 363.

We might see pałuba in this sense as a reflection of the aesthetic goals of Expressionism - that the artistic work be a direct expression of emotion, a precursor to Witkacy's theory of 'Pure Form' and, as Schulz observed in his review of *Ferdydurke,* a source of Gombrowicz's fascination with 'immaturity' or the raw core of desire concealed by fashion and social norms.[14]

Among the interwar Polish-avantgarde, the central question is that of 'form', and this *pałuba* might be the beginning of a Schulzian theory of form. The struggle for 'form' is joined most stridently by Witkacy with his theory of 'Pure Form', which is not exactly form as distinct from 'content' as one might associate with 'purity', but a kind of artistic representation that can be taken in whole and without mediation, producing 'the metaphysical feeling of the strangeness of existence'. This idea is rooted most deeply in the theory of the Sublime, but perhaps more immediately in the aesthetics of Expressionism - the idea that a painting like Edward Munch's *The Scream* is not a representation of a man screaming into the fjord, but is in fact itself a scream. The key theorist of Expressionism was the Polish writer of the literary generation before Witkacy and Schulz, Stanisław Przybyszewski who wrote the text for Munch's first Berlin exhibition and is said to have suggested the concrete name *The Scream* for Munch's most famous painting, over Munch's original emotive title, *Despair.*[15] Witkacy argued that poetry, painting, and drama were capable of Pure Form, while prose in general could at best only represent the experience of the individual in the face of Pure Form - the exception being the prose of Bruno Schulz, which possessed this quality of poetry for Witkacy.

In Schulz the word figures most prominently in the *Treatise on Tailor's Dummies* (Traktat o manekinach). As the father articulates his theory of matter and form, he states,

> The Demiurge, that great master and artist, made [matter] invisible, made it disappear under the play of life. We, on the contrary, love its creak, its resistance, its *pałubiasta* clumsiness[16]

Again the elusive hag, here as an adjective, is lost in the English translation. This *pałuba* cast here in the adjective form, *pałubiasta,* offers its own creak

14 B. Schulz in *Opowiadania...* op. cit., p. 389.

15 R. Heller, *Munch: His Life and Work*, University of Chicago Press, Chicago, 1984, p. 130.

16 B. Schulz in *Opowiadania...* op. cit., p. 36.

(zgrzyt), resistance (oporność), and clumsiness (niezgrabność). This word frustrates Schulz's translators precisely because it introduces the element of defamiliarization that Irzykowski found in it some thirty-odd years earlier.

An interesting analogue to *pałuba* might be the word 'fetish', which has certainly become the worn coin that Irzykowski was attempting to avoid, through repeated use in Marxist and Freudian contexts. To understand the rhetorical power, however, of Marx's and later Freud's use of the term, we need to defamiliarize it by recalling its original sense from nineteenth-century ethnography. A fetish is originally a doll or object that carries spiritual power not inherent in the material of the object itself. When blues singers like Muddy Waters and Junior Wells sing, "I'm goin' down to Louisiana, to get me a mojo hand", they are referring to a spice bag that was thought to bestow sexual power on the wearer. This is a fetish. So when Marx refers to 'commodity fetishism', he is saying that capitalists are like primitives ascribing mystical power to iron, coal, and pork bellies. Freud, writing in the context of modernist primitivism, borrows from this underlying primitivistic analogy in his analysis of psychological sexual fetishism. By the time Schulz is writing his stories, the word 'fetish' had lost its original primitivist mana, but pałuba retains this spiritual power to this day.

A few pages later in his description of the waxwork figures in a 'panopticon' or carnival sideshow, the author of the treatise asks,

> Can you imagine the pain, the dull imprisoned suffering, hewn into the matter of that pałuba which does not know why it must be what it is, why it must remain in that forcibly imposed form which is no more than a parody?[17]

The published English version renders pałuba here as 'dummy' and the French version as 'idole'. This is not the 'dummy' (manekin, mannequin) of the title, but a powerful effigy, commensurate with the inchoate power of matter imprisoned in form. The contrast between the material reality of the wax figures and their 'forcibly imposed form' is very much analogous to Irzykowski's contrast between the 'pałubic element' and the 'cloak' of accepted social norms that conceal the reality of life.

Father refers to these figures three more times as *pałuby*.

[17] ibid., p. 38.

> From this flows, gentlemen, the terrible sadness of all the jesting golems, of all the pałuby, brooding tragically on their funny grimaces.[18]

The golem of course is a monster of Jewish myth - a figure of coarse features like a *pałuba,* recast in late versions as a superhuman figure who rescues the Jews from persecution, and seen by some contemporary scholars as the model for comic book characters like Superman.

> Later Father asks,

> Is there in this pałuba truly anything of Queen Draga, her double, or even the remotest shadow of her existence?[19]

He goes on to acknowledge that the name 'Queen Draga' carries more meaning than the figure. It is perhaps acknowledged that the tale of the Serbian common woman who married King Aleksandr Obrenovic, both killed in a conflict over succession to the Serbian throne in 1903, had begun to fade into obscurity by the time of Schulz's stories.

These waxwork figures are *pałuby* of a very interesting sort. They are cast from underlying stories. The wax museum might be seen as another form of *The Booke,* Schulz's *Xięga,* or perhaps as a collection like Schulz's stamp album, rendered in three dimensions. Imprisoned in each figure is a substrate of mythic narrative - like the lost tale of the golem or the forgotten story of Queen Draga - which is reality for Schulz, as we would recognize from the frequently quoted passage in his essay, *The Mythicization of Reality:*

> Every fragment of reality lives by virtue of partaking in a universal sense[20].... Poetry happens when short-circuits of sense occur between words, a sudden regeneration of the primeval myths.... Not one scrap of an idea of ours does not originate in myth, isn't transformed, mutilated, denatured mythology. The most fundamental function of the spirit is

[18] ibid., p. 39.

[19] ibid., p. 39.

[20] I have chosen not to capitalize 'sense,' as it is not capitalized in the original text. My ellipses.

> inventing fables, creating tales.... [T]he building materials [that the search for human knowledge] uses were used once before; they come from forgotten, fragmented tales or "histories". Poetry recognizes these lost meanings, restores words to their places, connects them by the old semantics.[21]

Draga's story is after all a fairly conventional tale - the commoner who marries a king. Like many fairy tales it ends darkly. The wax figure with its uncanny physical realism utterly fails to tell the story. Schulz's fiction restores the lost connection.

In the father's final reference to *pałuby* he hints at the other possible meaning of *pałuba*, related etymologically to 'kadłub', meaning the shell of a structure or the hull of a ship, or the alternate meaning of *pałuba* as the cab of a wagon.

> Have you heard at night the terrible howling of these waxen pałuby, shut up in the booths of the fair, the lamenting chorus of these hulls (kadłuby) of wood and porcelain, banging their fists on the walls of their prison?

The idea of the body as an empty shell, perhaps like a 'zombie', certainly resonates with Irzykowski's idea of the 'cloak' that conceals underlying reality, but it is a connection that Irzykowski leaves as implicit. Schulz again recovers lost meaning by bringing these words into proximity in a single sentence. We might ask whether this is what he meant all along, but the first reference to pałuby in the story *Autumn* unquestionably compares the clumps of burs to peasant dolls.

Aleksandr Brückner draws the connection in his etymological dictionary between 'kadłub' and the derogatory sense of *pałuba* to mean an 'old hag' by virtue of the idea of concealment or covering, referring perhaps to the head scarves associated with old women, or possibly referring to their bodies as empty 'hulks'. By Schulz's time this would have become a submerged metaphor, another worn coin in Irzykowski's sense, or perhaps a palimpsest. To look at the worn coin and defamiliarize it in this way brings the sunken meaning to the surface, in contrast to Sienkiewicz who uses the term in a way that relies

---

21 *Letters and Drawings of Bruno Schulz with Selected Prose,* ed. J. Ficowski, tr. W. Arndt with V. Nelson, Fromm, New York, 1990, pp. 115–116.

on layers of hidden implications below the surface to flesh out the colorful character who speaks such a word. We can see how both approaches are valid methods of artistic expression. For Sienkiewicz, the layers of submerged meaning contribute to Zawiłowski's overall gestalt. Schulz unmasks these hidden layers as a way of exploring forgotten narratives and adds a layer of complexity to Irzykowski's theory of the 'pałubic element'. Schulz's contribution to the struggle for form in the interwar period might be the notion that there is nothing that does not partake of sublimity when viewed through the 'poetic' imagination capable of identifying and reassembling the lost mythologies in any degraded scrap of reality.

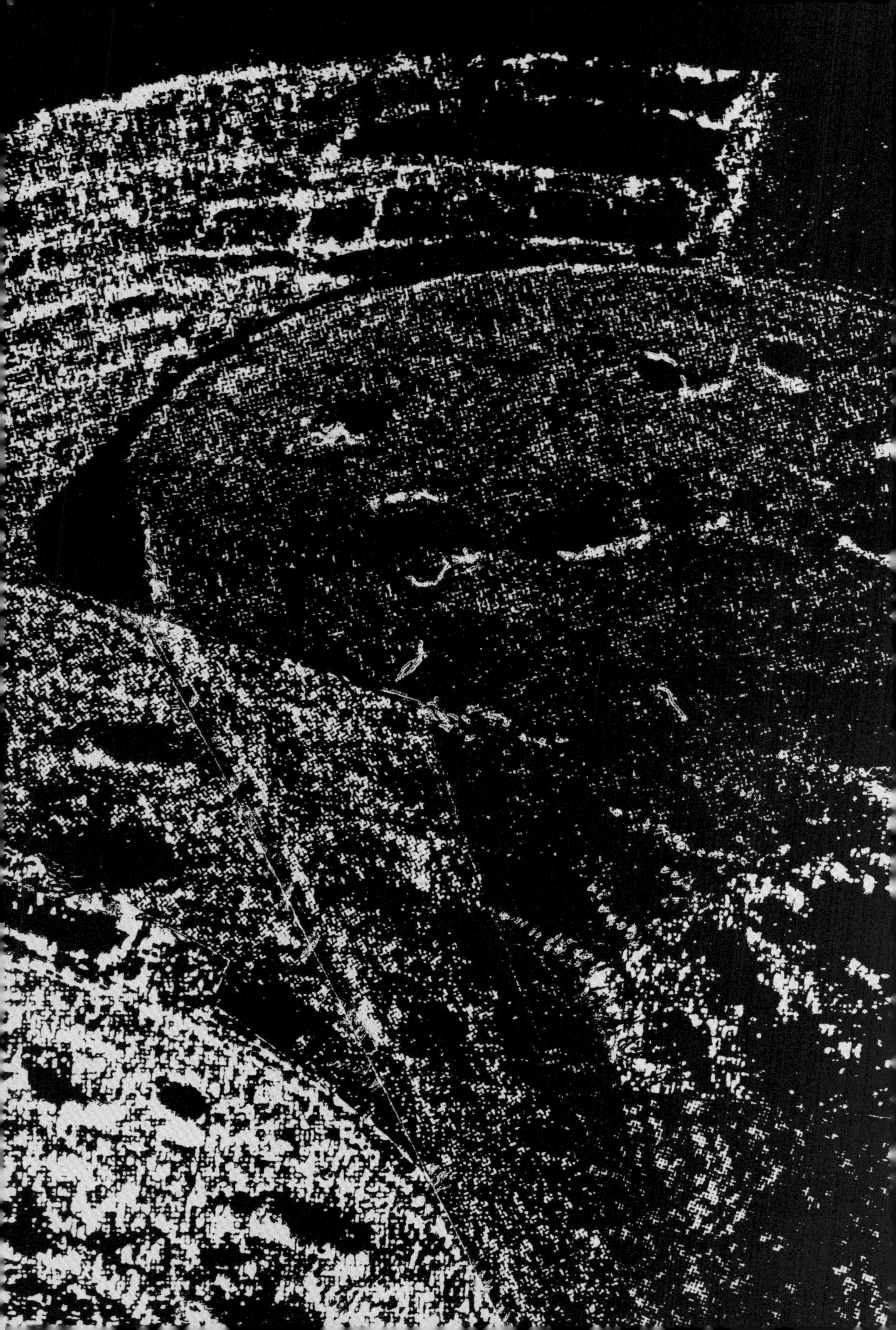

Le code métaphorique de Schulz sur l'exemple de la nouvelle la « Bourrasque »

Małgorzata Smorąg-Goldberg – Université Paris IV - Sorbonne, CIRCE (Centre Interdisciplinaire d'Études Centre-Européennes)

Resumé

Quel est le statut des textes schulziens ? Avons-nous véritablement à faire chez lui à un type d'écriture qui se situe aux antipodes de la transparence référentielle du témoignage, du compte-rendu factuel de la réalité.

À la lumière des récents travaux consacrés à l'imaginaire de Schulz (notamment la monographie de Krzysztof Stala, intitulée « Sur les marges de la réalité »), l'article de Małgorzata Smorąg-Goldberg revient à la question de la réalité et de son statut dans l'œuvre de Schulz. Elle y réfléchit, à partir de son exemple, à la problématique du codage métaphorique en littérature et à ses fonctions.

En posant les choses de façon la plus générale possible, l'auteur rappelle que l'on peut distinguer deux mécanismes du processus artistique : le mécanisme mimétique, avec deux cas de figure et le parti pris de l'anti-mimétisme. Pour ce qui est du premier, il se décline de la manière suivante : tout d'abord l'utopie de la transparence référentielle avec un rapport parfaitement identifiable au référent, autrement dit la description la plus « vraie » possible, la plus proche de la réalité des faits rapportés, avec une implication limitée de l'instance narrative. Nous sommes alors du côté du document-témoignage, mais qui grâce au travail de la sélection et de la composition peut devenir littérature. Et deuxièmement : tout ce qui se trouve du côté de la convention littéraire du témoignage où la marge de manœuvre de l'instance narrative augmente et où le pacte n'est plus celui de la « vérité » et de la fidélité absolue à un référent identifiable. C'est au contraire le choix de l'efficacité d'une construction/reconstruction fictive pour rendre au mieux compte du monde qui prévaut ici. Bien entendu, la frontière entre les deux n'est pas étanche.

L'article pose la question suivante : lorsque le rapport à un référent identifiable se réduit voire disparaît, au profit de la polysémie des lectures possibles, la dimension de témoignage disparaît-elle pour autant ? Ne peut-on pas trouver dans cette famille de textes, des témoignages qui ne témoignent pas d'un fait précis et identifiable mais qui postulent une dimension du monde en recourant à une forme d'allégorie de l'événement vécu.

*La spécificité et la profonde originalité du style de Schulz naissent justement de la tentative de réunir ce qui au début du XX*e *siècle sépare l'art en* *deux camps opposés. D'un côté l'obsession de nommer les sensations, les états affectifs et psychiques conscients ou inconscients à la recherche d'une forme d'authenticité du témoignage existentiel et de l'autre, l'art qui tend de plus en plus à s'autonomiser, à rompre toute obligation de représenter, à se tourner vers sa propre matière voire matérialité.*

Pour comprendre comment Schulz arrive à ménager des passerelles de l'un vers l'autre, comment son écriture donne à voir et témoigne d'une certaine réalité qui n'est jamais nommée et qui pourtant constitue le substrat existentiel de son être-au-monde, à savoir son judaïsme et la façon dont il affleure dans son écriture, l'article propose une relecture de sa nouvelle intitulée « La bourrasque » (« Wichura »).

Le point de départ de l'article part du postulat suivant : le rôle de la « Bourrasque » dans l'économie narrative du recueil est d'apporter un certain éclairage, une couleur affective au monde représenté, dans la mesure où la nouvelle « témoigne » du rapport à un arrière-plan omniprésent dans le sous-sol du texte schulzien, à savoir son judaïsme.

Selon l'auteur de l'article « La bourrasque » représente, le point central du rapport que les récits de Schulz entretiennent avec le référent qui constitue sa réalité quotidienne. Elle apparaît comme une sorte de mise en abyme, de métatexte fournissant la clef qui permet de comprendre comment Schulz révèle et dévoile, dans ses récits, le substrat sur lequel se fonde son monde et conséquemment son écriture.

L'article pose ainsi la question de la stratégie littéraire de Schulz-écrivain-juif-de-langue-polonaise en y répondant non du point de vue de l'histoire de la littérature en présentant l'arrière plan socioculturel de la Galicie de son enfance, mais en essayant de fournir des éléments de réponse textuelle pour éclairer de l'intérieur cette stratégie de l'entre-deux que pratique Schulz dans son écriture. En tordant le cou au stéréotype de la multiculturalité harmonieuse des confins galiciens, l'article tente de démontrer la force des oppositions et des conflits internes liés à ce genre de constructions identitaires, en montrant comment il affleure dans l'écriture de Schulz.

Ainsi en plaçant « La bourrasque » au cœur de la problématique des liens qu'entretient la fiction et la réalité, l'article propose de relire le texte comme une sorte de déclaration métaphorique de la judéité de Schulz, en passant par la tentative de dialogue, sur le terrain de l'écriture, avec un topos de la littérature juive à savoir la figure de la persécution, du pogrome. Il s'agirait donc d'une déclaration d'identité qui recouperait et rejoindrait son identité existentielle, celle d'un écrivain avant tout, en transcendant l'autre, celle culturelle, religieuse, ethnique. Comme s'il ne pouvait élaborer et construire cette déclaration autrement, lui l'écrivain, qu'en ayant recours aux codes de l'écriture.L'article propose de suivre sur l'exemple précis de « La bourrasque » comment l'image de la tempête, lieu commun au sens propre et figuré, c'est–à dire à la fois stéréotype éculé et lieu où Schulz communie avec les siens, est reprise et réinvestie par lui, pour être ensuite annexée à son imaginaire. L'oscillation entre le sens littéral et figuré, la superposition des deux et le constant va-et-vient de l'un à l'autre, sans cesse maintenus dans le texte, provoquent une sorte de contamination par l'image de l'obscurité/obscurantisme de toute la langue employée.

Le texte schulzien nous invite ainsi au décryptage, ce que révèle une sorte de surcondensation métaphorique des figures employées, accroissant ainsi l'épaisseur sémantique des mots, démultipliant leurs sens sous-jacents.

Les conclusions de l'article sont les suivantes : dans le cycle des Boutiques de cannelle Schulz pratique une sorte de rééquilibrage, de compensation, qui semble s'établir entre l'absence quasi complète des formes extérieures de judéité dans ses récits et la présence, foisonnante sitôt qu'on veut bien y prêter attention, des thèmes et des figures liés à une vision de la condition juive. Le mécanisme de cette alchimie, qui sait évoquer sans dire et transformer une apparente absence en fourmillante présence, n'est pas la moindre des réussites de l'écrivain Schulz. Il y a là, en effet, le résultat d'une longue réflexion sur la littérature.

Pour Schulz le véritable écrivain doit interposer entre son expérience et ses lecteurs, une grille, une forme de filtre. Par le biais de cette grille, l'écriture n'est plus soumise à la dictée de l'immédiateté de l'expérience, elle acquiert, au contraire, le pouvoir de créer des figures qui, pour des lecteurs à venir, peuvent contenir des significations nouvelles, parce qu'elles rendent possible l'actualisation d'un savoir hélas nouveau, pour nous le savoir de l'après Shoah.

Ainsi ce qui est en jeu dans le douloureux débat de Schulz avec sa judéité, ce n'est rien de moins que son image d'écrivain. L'art de Schulz ce fut de trouver la solution pour lui la plus signifiante à ce débat, correspondant à son identité d'artiste avant tout, donc une clef métaphorique.

Lorsque Witold Gombrowicz revient dans son Journal sur les liens qui le lient aux deux autres représentants de ce qu'il est convenu de considérer comme la trinité de l'avant-garde artistique et littéraire de la Pologne de l'entre-deux-guerres, à savoir Schulz et Witkacy, il écrit ceci :

> Mais nous formions malgré tout une trinité, et même assez caractéristique. Witkiewicz : affirmation délibérée des folies

> de la « forme pure » par le biais de la vengeance et pour que s'accomplisse le tragique du destin ; un fou désespéré. Schulz : absorption par la forme ; un fou noyé. Moi : tentative passionnée pour me frayer, à travers la forme, un chemin vers mon « moi » et la réalité; un fou révolté[1].

À travers cette formule lapidaire et simplificatrice, caractéristique de cette mauvaise foi que Gombrowicz pratiquait si souvent, ce dernier met cependant le doigt sur un problème crucial, à savoir le combat avec la forme, qui fut la préoccupation principale des recherches les plus intéressantes en littérature au cours du premier tiers du XXe siècle. C'est au nom de ce que l'on jugea être de l'ordre de l'excès de la forme qu'au lendemain de la seconde guerre mondiale, lorsque la revue *Twórczość* [2] (encore sous la direction de Kazimierz Wyka), en 1946, lança une enquête auprès des intellectuels et artistes polonais ouvrant ainsi une discussion sur le bilan de la littérature de l'entre-deux-guerres, la réponse fut unanimement négative.

Comme si les expériences de l'horreur pure, de mal absolu, rendaient radicalement caduc le codage littéraire. Comme s'il fallait revenir à une forme de voix blanche, celle du témoignage, du compte-rendu, seule façon désormais de restituer ce que, pour parler vite, on pourrait appeler la « désillusion humaniste ».

C'est là qu'il serait intéressant de reposer la question sur les moyens qu'a l'art en général et la littérature en particulier de témoigner. La métaphore, le codage artistique sont-ils « inconvenants » face à l'expérience du mal ?

Si l'on présente les choses de façon la plus générale possible, nous avons deux mécanismes du processus artistique : le mécanisme mimétique, avec deux cas de figure et le parti pris de l'anti-mimétisme. Pour ce qui est du premier, il se décline de la manière suivante : tout d'abord l'utopie de la transparence référentielle avec un rapport parfaitement identifiable au référent, autrement

---

1 Witold Gombrowicz, *Journal* t. II, folio, Paris 1995, traduction française revue et complétée par Dominique Autrand, Christophe Jeżewski et Allan Kosko 1959–69, p. 219-220 ; l'original polonais : „Ale byliśmy mimo wszystko trójcą i to dosyć charakterystyczną. Witkiewicz: umyślne afirmowanie szaleństw 'czystej formy' przez zemstę, a też żeby się wypełniły tragiczne przeznaczenia, wariat zrozpaczony. Schulz: zatracenie się w formie, wariat utopiony. Ja: żądza przebicia się poprzez formę do «ja» mojego i do rzeczywistości, wariat zbuntowany." *Dziennik 1961–66*, Instytut literacki, Paris 1984, p.17–18.

2 *Twórczość,* mensuel littéraire, créé en 1945, et dirigé successivement par Kazimierz Wyka, Jarosław Iwaszkiewicz et Jerzy Lissowski.

dit la description la plus « vraie » possible, la plus proche de la réalité des faits rapportés, avec une implication de l'instance narrative la plus limitée possible. Nous sommes alors plutôt du côté du document-témoignage, mais qui grâce au travail de la sélection, de la composition peut devenir littérature. Et deuxièmement : tout ce qui se trouve du côté de la convention littéraire du témoignage où la marge de manœuvre de l'instance narrative augmente et où le pacte n'est plus celui de la « vérité », de l'authenticité, de la fidélité absolue à un référent identifiable. C'est au contraire le choix de l'efficacité d'une construction/reconstruction fictive pour rendre au mieux compte du monde, qui prévaut ici. Bien entendu, la frontière entre les deux n'est pas étanche, voir le *Journal* de Gombrowicz, et l'utilisation de l'artifice littéraire pour créer « un effet de quotidienneté ».

C'est à partir de là, de l'impératif catégorique de l'expression, de l'expressivité aux dépens de la fidèle reproduction de la réalité que l'on passe du côté de l'anti-mimétisme et que tous les codes métaphoriques entrent en ligne de compte. Le rapport à un référent identifiable se réduit voire disparaît, au profit de la polysémie des lectures possibles (des différentes modalités de lecture pourrait-on dire).

Mais la dimension de témoignage disparaît-elle pour autant dans ce cas de figure ? Ne peut-on pas trouver dans cette famille de textes des témoignages qui ne témoignent pas d'un fait précis et identifiable au sens de témoigner de ..., d'attester, de rapporter, de reproduire ce qu'on a vu, entendu, perçu, servant à l'établissement de la vérité, mais au contraire des témoignages qui accréditent, postulent une dimension du monde au sens de rendre témoignage à ..., d'exprimer, de manifester, de donner à voir. Bref opter pour l'opération scripturale qui consiste à créer une forme d'allégorie de l'événement vécu.

Mais revenons à notre première citation de Gombrowicz et à cette question de **la forme et de ses excès** dans l'écriture de Bruno Schulz.

Il semblerait, à priori, que nous ayons à faire avec Schulz à un type d'écriture aux antipodes de la transparence référentielle du témoignage, du compte-rendu factuel de la réalité, aux antipodes d'une écriture débarrassée des fioritures de la forme jugée, au lendemain de la seconde guerre mondiale, comme décalée face aux expériences de ce maudit XXe siècle.

Au cours de la dernière décennie, il y eut toute une série de nouveaux travaux consacrés à l'imaginaire de Schulz et notamment une monographie de Krzysztof Stala, intitulée *Sur les marges de la réalité*[3], qui de façon remarquable

[3] K. Stala, *Na marginesach rzeczywistości*, Wydawnictwo Literackie, Kraków, 1998.

décortique les paradoxes de la représentation dans l'œuvre de Schulz. En prenant pour appui un certain nombre de thèses de Stala, il serait intéressant de revenir ainsi *à la question de la réalité et de son statut dans l'œuvre de Schulz* et de réfléchir sur son exemple à la problématique du codage, du cryptage métaphorique en littérature. Tout se passe comme si les expériences traumatiques de la deuxième moitié du XXe siècle, avaient eu pour fonction de radicaliser et de rendre plus lisibles les mécanismes littéraires inhérents, de tout temps, au fait d'écrire, c'est-à-dire au processus de refiguration et de transmission d'une expérience du monde.

Il est incontestable que les recherches artistiques les plus intéressantes du XXe siècle ont pour fondement la crise de la représentation qui lui sert de prélude. C'est elle qui détermina ce que l'on appelle le tournant moderniste. C'est elle qui aiguillonnait, à l'époque, l'intérêt croissant des artistes pour les processus de codage artistique, la mise en avant de tout ce qui serait, disons, du côté de l'anti-mimésis, c'est-à-dire d'une part du côté du symbole et du mythe et de l'autre de la matérialité du mot, de la substance palpable de la langue poétique, du « grain de la voix » dans la narration. Bref, la crise de la représentation qui ouvre le XXe siècle, ouvre du même coup le débat, autour de ce qui fonde les mécanismes de la représentation tout court. Cela dit, la poursuite de la réalité ne cesse d'être l'horizon d'attente de toutes ces recherches, même si elles s'incarnent surtout dans des formes négatives et radicales, dans des gestes de violente opposition.

Nous sommes avec l'écriture de Schulz au cœur-même des questions que se pose l'art au XXe siècle. Comment adapter les formes de représentation de la réalité au sentiment de la perte de repères, de l'émiettement de la réalité, de l'apparition de l'intérêt pour ce que l'auteur des *Boutiques de cannelle* nomme le réservoir honteux « des produits occasionnels, accidentels, des rebuts de processus culturels, une zone de contenus sub-culturels, incultes, rudimentaires, une zone immense de déchets qui encombrent les périphéries de la culture »[4]? Quelles sont les formes que revêt la « folle poursuite de la Réalité » demande Schulz, à un moment où l'art et la littérature, encore confiants en leur pouvoir, donc avant Auschwitz et Kołyma, pour utiliser là aussi des noms de code, cherchent à s'auto-analyser et à s'auto-définir ? C'est

4 *Gombrowicz,* L'Herne, Paris 1971, p. 48 ; L'original polonais: „pewne uboczne i odpadkowe produkty procesów kulturalnych, strefa treści podkulturalnych, niedokształconych i rudymentarnych, ogromne rumowisko kultury zaśmiecające jej peryferie", in *Gombrowicz i krytycy,* p. 51, Wydawnictwo Literackie, Kraków, 1984.

de cette faille qui scinde au début du XXe siècle l'art en deux camps opposés, que naît la spécificité et la profonde originalité du style de Schulz. D'un côté, ce qui continue à demeurer le moteur fondamental de l'écriture pour tous ces artistes, à savoir l'obsession de nommer : les sensations, les états affectifs et psychiques conscients ou inconscients, de sonder les fondements de l'univers à la recherche toujours et encore, d'une forme d'authenticité du témoignage existentiel et de l'autre, l'art qui tend de plus en plus à s'autonomiser, à rompre toute attache, toute obligation de représenter, à se tourner vers sa propre matière voire matérialité – la langue – à descendre dans son territoire propre unique et singulier, bref à déplacer la passion de connaître de l'extérieur vers l'intérieur, vers sa substance même.

Pour comprendre comment Schulz arrive à ménager des passerelles de l'un vers l'autre, comment une certaine réalité qui n'est jamais nommée et qui pourtant constitue le substrat existentiel de son être-au-monde affleure dans son écriture, je voudrais vous proposer une relecture de sa nouvelle intitulée « La bourrasque » (Wichura)[5]. Plus qu'une série d'affirmations ou de révélations sur la « Bourrasque », cette analyse se voudrait être un inventaire des questions que je me pose à son sujet.

Il serait donc intéressant de réfléchir tout d'abord à sa fonction dans le cycle narratif des *Boutiques de cannelle* puis de formuler une hypothèse. En effet, cette nouvelle apparaît comme le point central du rapport que les récits de Schulz entretiennent avec le référent qui constitue sa réalité quotidienne. Elle apparaît comme une sorte de mise en abyme, de méta-texte fournissant la clef qui permet de comprendre comment Schulz révèle et dévoile, dans ses récits, le substrat sur lequel se fonde son monde et conséquemment son écriture. Je voudrais parler ici de la question de la judéité de Schulz, du rapport entre son écriture et la réalité à laquelle elle renvoie, entre le texte et son contexte, bref entre la textualité et la référentialité.

Dans la configuration du cycle des *Boutiques de cannelle,* la « Bourrasque » occupe, à mon avis, une place à part. Elle n'apporte rien ni du point de vue de l'organisation de l'intrigue, ni de la conduite du récit, ni non plus du point de vue de la poursuite d'une série d'aventures du héros avec le monde. Elle est courte, constituée de cinq pages, pourtant il y a dans le recueil des nouvelles qui sont plus courtes encore („Pan" : 3 pages, „Pan Karol" : 3 pages, „Karakony" – 4 pages), ce n'est donc pas le seul fait de sa brièveté qui l'isole de l'ensemble.

[5] B. Schulz, « La bourrasque » dans *Les boutiques de cannelle,* traduit en français par G. Lissowski, Denoël, Paris, 1974.

Son rôle dans l'économie narrative du recueil est d'apporter un certain éclairage, une couleur affective au monde représenté. Parce qu'elle « témoigne », au sens de manifester - me semble-t-il - du rapport à un arrière-plan omniprésent dans le sous-sol du texte schultzien, à savoir son judaïsme.

Parmi les travaux qui ont apporté des nouveaux éclairages de l'œuvre de Schulz, en dehors de la monographie de Krzysztof Stala, déjà mentionnée, il y a eu deux volumes d'articles parus dans la continuité des commémorations du 100e anniversaire de la naissance de Schulz et du 50e anniversaire de sa mort: *In mémoriam*[6] et *Czytanie Schulza*[7] (de Jerzy Jarzębski). Dans l'article d'Eugenia Prokop-Janiec[8], publié dans le volume intitulé *Czytanie Schulza,* celle-ci pose la question de la stratégie littéraire de Schulz-écrivain-juif-de-langue-polonaise. Elle y répond en historienne de la littérature en présentant l'arrière plan socio-culturel de la Galicie de son enfance et de ce qui en est resté dans la Pologne de l'entre-deux-guerres et le met en perspective avec les choix identitaires représentés par un Leśmian d'un coté et un Tuwim ou Słonimski de l'autre[9]. Dans ce qu'elle appelle la stratégie littéraire de l'écrivain juif de langue polonaise (pisarz polskojęzyczny o rodowodzie żydowskim) entre avant tout la façon dont il répond à la question suivante : si et dans l'affirmative, de quelle manière, l'expérience du judaïsme transparaît dans son écriture ? Elle distingue alors trois catégories : l'assimilation excessive, désormais assez rare dans la Pologne de l'entre-deux-guerres (de type Leśmian) ; l'assimilation modérée, la plus rependue (représentée par un Tuwim, par exemple) et le courant national-juif, qui commence à se faire jour à l'époque (de type Roman Brandstaetter). En éclairant le milieu fréquenté par Schulz, sa collaboration occasionnelle aux revues juives de langue polonaise, la place qui y était réservée à son œuvre, le milieu fréquenté par Schulz au quotidien qui, en dehors de ses rares visites à Varsovie[10] et de ses échanges épistolaires, était essentiellement composé d'intelligentsia juive, elle met le doit sur une forme de contradiction liée à son sentiment d'appartenance. On pourrait rappeler ici ce qu'en dit Henri Lewi, le biographe français de Schulz : « A l'égard de la Pologne, Schulz se veut et s'affirme dedans en réalité et massivement il est

6 Małgorzata Kitowska-Łysiak (red.), *In memoriam,* FIS, Lublin, 1994.

7 Jerzy Jarzębski (réd.), *Czytanie Schulza,* Oficyna Naukowa i Literacka, Kraków, 1994.

8 Eugenia Prokop-Janiec, „Schulz a galicyjski tygiel kultur" dans *Czytanie Schulza,* op. cit., p. 95–107.

9 Eugenia Prokop-Janiec, ibid., p. 85.

10 Il y noue des relations avec Zofia Nałkowska, Tadeusz Breza, Witold Gombrowicz, Stanisław Ignacy Witkiewicz.

dehors. A l'égard des Juifs, Schulz manifeste son extériorité, mais il est facile de voir qu'il est dedans »[11].

Je voudrais réfléchir à cette question en la replaçant dans la problématique du rapport entre fiction et témoignage, c'est-à-dire en essayant de fournir des éléments de réponse textuelle. D'où la relecture de ce texte comme une sorte de déclaration métaphorique de la judéité de Schulz, passant par la tentative de dialogue, sur le terrain de l'écriture, avec un topos de la littérature juive à savoir la figure de la persécution, du pogrome. C'est donc une déclaration d'identité qui recoupe et rejoint son identité existentielle, celle de l'écrivain en transcendant l'autre, celle culturelle, religieuse, ethnique, comme on veut, comme s'il ne pouvait élaborer et construire cette déclaration autrement, lui l'écrivain, qu'en ayant recours aux codes de l'écriture.

Un mot encore sur la terminologie ici employée : j'entends par judéité à la fois le fait d'être juif (judéité objective) et la manière de l'être (judéité subjective), or c'est la distance de l'une à l'autre qui est dans le cas de Schulz, productrice de sens.

Encore une précision, la nouvelle dont il sera question est déterritorialisée par rapport à un contexte historique identifiable (un pogrome précis) ou biographique (ce que Schulz enfant aurait pu voir ou subir) et pourtant elle nous atteint non seulement par ses contenus latents et souterrains, mais parce qu'elle touche à la dynamique des apprentissages (l'expérience du mal, de la violence, du déchaînement de la force hostile).

À la limite, la question de savoir si Schulz a été ou pas le témoin direct des persécutions est subsidiaire ici. Il est vrai cependant que le départ de toute la famille pour Vienne au moment des troubles liés à la première guerre mondiale, peut s'expliquer dans ce contexte-là. Ce qui nous importe, c'est qu'il se solidarise - sur le terrain de l'écriture - avec l'expérience des siens : et là on peut citer le boycotte des commerces juifs voté par le Congrès catholique de Cracovie en 1893 - une des raisons possibles de la faillite de la boutique paternelle, puis la vague des persécutions antisémites au moment de la guerre polono-soviétique sur ces terrains-là (décrites par Babel dans son *Journal*[12], etc.)

Cela dit, le moins que l'on puisse dire, c'est que dans la fiction schulzienne proprement dite, la référence juive, le thème juif, ne prolifèrent pas. Dans ses récits, ayant tous pourtant, pour point de départ, son Drohobycz natal, dont la population en 1939 comptait 15.000 juifs, ce qui représentait 40 % de sa

---

11 Voir H. Lewi, *Bruno Schulz*, Criterion, Paris, 1995, p. 57.

12 I. Babel, *Cavalerie Rouge*, suivi de *Journal de 1920*, Acte Sud, Paris 1998.

population totale, le mot 'juif' ne paraît presque pas. On le trouve une fois, pour évoquer un Sanhédrin, bien éloigné des masses juives de Galicie (dans « La nuit de la grande saison »), nulle part dans ses lettres[13]. Pour un auteur dont l'un des procédés favoris est la récurrence, la saturation, le retour obsessionnel du motif, il y a là un souci de la litote qui mérite d'être relevé. On se souviendra qu'une remarque du même ordre peut être faite à propos de Kafka, qui sur ce point avait poussé encore plus loin sa discrétion puisque le mot juif n'apparaît nulle part dans ses œuvres !

Sur l'exemple de la « Bourrasque », je voudrais montrer pourtant certaines traces ou affleurements de ce substrat juif qui chez Schulz ne sont pas toujours là où on les attend ou encore là où il les exhibe explicitement.

Tout d'abord le titre « La bourrasque » (« Wichura »), entre en résonance avec toute la tradition juive de récits de persécution. En effet, parler d'une irruption soudaine de violence antisémite en utilisant des images de tempête, de bourrasque et autres synonymes d'intempéries, fait partie du réservoir traditionnel des figures élaborées par des récits de persécution au cours du XIXe siècle jusqu'à la première guerre mondiale. Cela concerne notamment les marges occidentales de l'empire russe – l'Ukraine et la Biélorussie entre autres - où étant donné la censure exercée par les autorités tsaristes, le recours à un style allusif était devenu la norme de l'épistolographie juive. Nous en trouvons des preuves dans la correspondance privée et dans la littérature yiddish lorsque celle-ci à recours au document épistolaire stylisé, pour s'assurer une caution d'authenticité. Je pourrais notamment citer une nouvelle de Sholem-Aleikhem, l'un des fondateurs de la littérature yiddish, dans une période de persécutions, de pogromes et d'exode pour les juifs de l'empire tsariste. Il s'agit de la nouvelle intitulée « La grande panique des petits bonshommes », extraite du recueil *Gens de Kasrilevké*[14]. La nouvelle commence par l'arrivé d'une lettre par laquelle les habitants du village, où se déroule l'action, apprennent l'irruption d'un pogrome dans la bourgade voisine et la lettre utilise précisément ce type de formulation, je cite :

---

[13] La référence est plus fréquente dans son œuvre graphique : *Le jeune homme juif et deux femmes*, 1918 ; *La rencontre*, l'huile, 1920 (où la tête du jeune juif est un autoportrait).

[14] Sholem-Aleikhem, *Gens de Kasrilevké*, trad. du yiddish et préf. Par Jacques Mandelbaum, Paris, Juillard, 1992, col. de littérature yiddish, (les récits qui composent le recueil on été publiés en feuilleton autour de l'année 1940), la nouvelle « La grande panique des petits bonshommes » se trouve à la p. 83-134 du présent volume.

> Ainsi vous faut-il savoir que le temps a bien changé par chez nous au point qu'une main d'homme et une plume d'oie ne sont pas de force à vous décrire cela. Toutefois nous sommes tous, Dieu en soit loué, en bonne santé [...] quoique encore **sous le coup de la grêle et de la tempête qui se sont abattus ici.**

Essayons de voir comment cette image de tempête, lieu commun au sens propre et figuré, c'est-à-dire à la fois stéréotype éculé et lieu où Schulz communie avec les siens, est reprise et réinvestie par lui, pour être ensuite annexée à son imaginaire. La phrase qui ouvre le récit met en place le paradigme de l'obscurité sinon de l'obscurantisme, des ténèbres qui d'abord s'amassent dans les greniers des maisons, pour ensuite exploser et déferler en foule compacte (la récurrence de la foule, de la populace déchaînée est omniprésente dans le passage) :

> Pendant ce long hiver vide l'obscurité recueillit dans notre ville une moisson centuplée[15].

L'oscillation entre le sens littéral et figuré, la superposition des deux et le constant va-et-vient de l'un à l'autre sont sans cesse maintenus dans le texte, ce qui provoque une sorte de contamination progressive de toute la langue employée. L'image se développe, son sens métaphorique se creuse, s'approfondit :

> L'obscurité se mit lentement à dégénérer et à fermenter sauvagement[16].

Puis viennent des images de plus en plus explicites : « sombres diètes » czarne sejmy, « débats bruyants et vains » (wiecowania gadatliwe), « bouillonnements fétides » (bełkotliwe flaszkowania), en polonais leur charge métaphorique est infiniment plus forte. Avec l'antropomorphisation des bouteilles, qui deviennent agents des actions à commettre, tout une chaîne d'associations de mots et d'images se met en place, liée aux scènes de beuverie et de violences

---

15 B. Schulz, op. cit. , p. 133; l'original polonais : « Tej długiej i pustej zimy obrodziła ciemność w naszym mieście ogromnym, stokrotnym urodzajem », « Wichura » dans *Sklepy cynamonowe*, Wydawnictwo Literackie, Kraków, 1985, p. 103.

16 ibid., p. 133; l'original polonais : « [...] ciemność zaczęła się wyradzać i dziko fermentować », ibid., p. 103.

commises sous l'effet de l'alcool, à la sortie de l'auberge, puis le passage culmine par cette phrase :

> Enfin une certaine nuit, les cohortes de casseroles et de bouteilles rassemblées firent éclater les toitures et déferlèrent **en une grande foule serrée** sur la ville[17].

Ce que Lissowski traduit par les cohortes est exprimé de façon beaucoup plus forte et en même temps plus explicite en polonais par « falangi garnków i flaszek ». Tout un paradigme de militarisation progressive de la foule se met d'ailleurs en place : nous avons « phalangistes », « armée », « colonnes ». Puis progressivement, comme si la description obéissait à un scénario bien codé, à l'évocation de la bêtise, de la masse et de la force (« C'est alors que débordèrent les grands fleuves noirs » que les « noirs assemblées bruyantes assiégèrent la ville ») se joint le déferlement des injures :

> leurs langues de bois moulaient dans leur bouche de bois un gargouillis d'imprécations et d'injures, éclaboussant de boue tout l'espace de la nuit. Et, à force de jurons et de blasphèmes, ils eurent enfin gain de cause[18].

La tempête durera trois jours et trois nuits. Le déroulement des événements obéira à un protocole bien codé : 'Tu n'iras pas à l'école aujourd'hui' dit la mère, l'enfant-narrateur court à la fenêtre pour regarder au dehors et le récit se déroule désormais en suivant la perspective du témoin muet et impuissant devant le spectacle observé à travers la vitre. Le monde surgit ainsi par le regard de celui qui observe. La figure du témoin, effaré par les événements auxquels il assiste, est d'ailleurs renforcée et répétée par la métaphore suivante :

---

[17] ibid., p. 133, op. cit.; l'original polonais: „Aż pewnej nocy wezbrały pod gontowymi przestworami falangi garnków i flaszek i popłynęły wielkim stłoczonym ludem na miasto", op. cit. p. 103.

[18] ibid., p. 134; l'original polonais : « I wszystkie kołatały niezgrabnie kołkami drewnianych języków, mełły nieudolnie w drewnianych gębach bełkot klątw i obelg, bluźniąc błotem na całej przestrzeni nocy. Aż dobluźniły się, doklęły swego », ibid. p. 103.

> Les grands hêtres autour de l'église levaient les bras au ciel, témoins de révélations bouleversantes et criaient, criaient[19].

Une sorte de contamination de l'effroi s'opère dans l'univers environnant par le biais du regard de l'enfant qui cherche des alliés dans le paysage familier de sa ville, mais les seuls témoins de l'horreur sont des arbres et non des hommes, qui adressent un cri muet au ciel. Cette image est d'une force extrême. La suite des événements se déroule selon un scénario bien codé : le feu apparaît :

> Vers deux heures de l'après-midi, un incendie éclata dans un faubourg et se propagea dangereusement. Ma mère et Adèle se mirent à emballer linge, fourrures et argenteries[20].
>
> Le feu se propageant, les préparatifs de l'exode se mettent en place.

On pourrait me rétorquer que je suis dans ma lecture victime d'une illusion rétrospective, qu'il y a eu entre temps la Shoah, qui induit un certain nombre d'associations d'images et impose un réservoir de motifs, un certain protocole du déroulement du récit de persécution. Je pourrais répondre ici que c'est justement le triomphe de la métaphore *in abstentia,* de la polysémie de ses ingrédients qui rendent possible cette lecture métahistorique. Chez Schulz, la métaphore est tout autre chose qu'une figure de rhétorique, elle ouvre, car elle est, comme chez Proust, un moyen d'approcher et de retenir l'acuité du réel et de lui conférer des sens dont l'avenir de l'expérience humaine et donc **des lectures à venir** est porteur. D'où ces phrases à cinq voire six mots, en apparence hétérogènes et disparates, mais qui, chacun renvoyant à un sens s'équivalent les uns les autres comme autant de tentatives pour capturer un moment où notre sensibilité a été entièrement et globalement affectée par un événement singulier. La métaphore est l'acte même de l'accomplissement dans le langage d'une opération que la sensation (la perception) ne sait pas

19 ibid., p. 136,; l'original polonais : « Ogromne buki koło kościoła stały z wzniesionymi rękami jak świadkowie wstrząsających objawień, i krzyczały, krzyczały ». ibid., p. 104.

20 ibid., p. 136, ; l'original polonais : « Około drugiej po południu wybuchł na przedmieściu pożar i rozszerzał się gwałtownie. Matka z Adelą zaczęły pakować pościel, futra i kosztowności ». ibid., p. 104.

encore tout à fait nommer, la trace d'un parcours qu'elle est en train d'effectuer entre le fait d'éprouver et la manière d'en rendre compte. Comme si la métaphore tirait sa vigueur de la fulgurance grâce à laquelle elle parvient à rejoindre l'événement d'une sensation qui n'est pas encore devenu savoir, et le pouvoir de l'expression à révéler cette sensation à elle-même et à lui frayer une voie vers la connaissance.

Cela dit, le récit « La Bourrasque », comme toujours chez Schulz, à partir d'une expérience singulière - l'initiation au déferlement de la violence extérieure vécue par le narrateur enfant-, expérience qui pourrait conférer au monde une structure binaire, simple, rassurante, le diviser en deux, nous et eux, victimes et bourreaux, dehors et dedans, se déplace, le propos se généralise, conduisant à une réflexion sur l'essence du mal et ses structures profondes. Là où, au départ, Schulz semble emprunter l'un des topos du réservoir traditionnel des figures élaborées par les récits des persécution de la littérature juive, là même, l'instant d'après, il prend ses distances avec cette vision du monde. Chez Sholem-Aleikhem toujours, par exemple dans *Tevié le laitier*[21] (qui plus tard deviendra le livret du *Violon sur le toit*), les persécutions soudent la communauté ; à un dehors inquiétant s'oppose un dedans rassurant. La cuisine qui sent bon la cannelle et la hala, avec ses préparatifs du shabbat devient un refuge douillet. Mais chez Schultz, il n'y a pas de salut, le mal est partout. En une phrase brève, la cuisine claire et rassurante où « Adèle pilait de la cannelle dans un mortier en fonte[22] », se trouve reliée au grenier, le siège des pulsions noires et inconscientes :

> « Nous étions assis dans la cuisine claire et éclairée. Derrière la cuisinière et la corniche noire de suie de la cheminée, un escalier conduisait au grenier[23] ».

La cuisine n'est pas coupée, séparée, épargnée, elle est reliée aux sources du mal, elle peut tout à coup aussi basculer dans les chaos, devenir le théâtre de

---

[21] Sholem-Aleikhem, *Tévié le laitier,* trad. par Colette Stoïanov et Dora Sanadzé, préf. de Charles Dobrzyński, dessins de Ilex Beller, Paris, Messidor, 1991. col. *Les grands romans de la liberté.*

[22] p. 139, op. cit. ; l'original polonais : « Adela tłukła cynamon w dźwięcznym moździerzu » op. cit. p. 107.

[23] p. 139, op. cit. ; l'original polonais : « Siedzieliśmy w jasno oświetlonej kuchni. Za ogniskiem kuchennym i czarnym, szerokim okapem komina prowadziło parę stopni do drzwi strychu ». op. cit. p. 107.

la violence, d'une violence qui vient de l'intérieur, qui vient des siens. « Tante Pérasie vint en visite » [Ciotka Perazja przyszła z wizytą]. **Et là :**

> « Tante Pérasie se déchaîna et déversa sur nous tout un flot d'injures. Folle de colère, elle vitupérait contre Adèle et ma mère à grand renfort des gestes. J'avais peine à comprendre de quoi il s'agissait, mais elle s'enferrait de plus en plus dans sa furie et ne fut bientôt plus qu'une boule d'insulte et de gesticulation[24]. »

La tante Pérasie, l'image est extraordinaire, « se décompose, se démembre en mille araignées, en mille cloportes parcourant en tous sens le plancher » pour finir par se consumer, rapetisser et s'autodétruire dans un accès de colère, à laquelle le narrateur et les siens assistent impuissants. Cette fin est énigmatique et en même temps extrêmement éloquente quant au territoire où il est vraiment chez lui est celui de l'écriture.

Le texte schulzien nous invite ainsi au décryptage, ce que révèle une sorte de surcondensation métaphorique des figures employées, accroissant ainsi l'épaisseur sémantique des mots, démultipliant leurs sens sous-jacents. Dans le matériau de la langue schulzienne nous observons ainsi ce jeu constant entre le sens littéral et le sens figuré : entre l'obscure (« ciemny ») et le noir (« czarny »). Tout cela au service d'une sorte de méta-description de l'expérience du mal. Ce processus de métaphorisation de la langue employée où les sens propres et figurés se contaminent, où une tension se crée de l'un à l'autre, la métaphore s'approchant et s'éloignant du référent qu'elle transpose, participe de la construction d'une allégorie de l'expérience du monde ici décrite : le déferlement de la violence pure.

La langue artistique de Schulz peut être considérée comme une forme d'écran qui à la fois voile et dévoile l'objet qui se trouve derrière et du même coup devient le moteur même de sa création.

Krzysztof Stala place Schulz entre le surréalisme et la méta-fiction : saisir et reproduire la réalité d'un côté et dévoiler sa structure profonde, la logique même de sa constitution de l'autre. Schulz pratique systématiquement le choc des deux systèmes de représentation. D'un côté une prose qui mime l'objectivité du reportage et de l'autre un chiffre poétique qui s'arroge tous

[24] p. 139-140, op. cit. ; l'original polonais : « Ciotka Perazja zaczęła się kłócić, kląć i złorzeczyć. » op. cit. p. 107.

les droits[25]. D'un côté la domination de « l'effet de réalité », fondé sur une reproduction fidèle de la réalité et de l'autre les lois de l'expression poétique : la remise en question de l'identité des lieux, de la linéarité des distances, de la cohérence temporelle.

Pour revenir à l'objet de notre étude : le rapport de Schulz au substrat juif de Drohobycz, le théâtre de son existence. C'est une sorte de rééquilibrage, de compensation, qui semble s'être établi entre l'absence quasi complète des formes extérieures de judéité dans ses récits et la présence, foisonnante sitôt qu'on veut bien y prêter attention, des thèmes et des figures liés à une vision de la condition juive. Le mécanisme de cette alchimie, qui sait évoquer sans dire et transformer une apparente absence en fourmillante présence, n'est pas la moindres des réussites de l'écrivain Schulz. Il y a là, en effet, le résultat d'une longue réflexion sur la littérature.

Ce principe d'écriture, cette idée que le véritable écrivain doit interposer entre son expérience et ses lecteurs, une grille, Schulz ne l'abandonnera jamais. Par le biais de cette grille, l'écriture n'est plus soumise à la dictée de l'expérience. Ainsi ce qui est en jeu dans le douloureux débat de Schulz avec sa judéité, ce n'est rien de moins que son image d'écrivain. L'art de Schulz ce fut de trouver la solution pour lui la plus signifiante à ce débat, correspondant à son identité d'artiste avant tout.

25 Voir Jean-Yves Tadié, *Le récit poétique,* PUF, Paris, 1978.

The Republic of Dreams: Town in Schulz's creation and interpretation

Vira Meniok – Ivan Franko Drohobycz State Pedagogical University

Abstract

The Town in Schulz's creative work is a universe of his art: from things that are the most important to things that are the most insignificant, fragmentary and changeable. For the Master it is a place of creation and of creative act. In a sense, Schulz's creative work is an original act of Town; it is an unfinished text about Town that did not fit all the pages of his written works. This phenomenon is not connected with real determinants of Drohobycz and its history – Schulz's mythologized, mystical and even sacral infinity of Town is always authentic.

'The chosen land, 'peculiar province', 'the town unique in all the world' are Schulz's categories of primary sense of Town. These are categories of eternity as they speak expressively about selectiveness, exclusiveness and uniqueness of that town, which, though is a province, ceases to be a province, overgrows itself, its real dimensions of a small town and experiences (thanks to Schulz) the act of ascension and becomes a piece of eternity. The biblical country Canaan becomes a sign of this "peculiar province", that is why for Schulz his town is the Promised Land, which he has brilliantly interpreted, but at the same time he is not its creator. He received the primary sense at the beginning of his life, and he never revealed it.

The narrator of The Republic of Dreams, a dreamer named Józef, unlike Schulz attempts to be a creator of genius and of this world built in his own way. He does it, when he lacks the energy of the interpreter, to understand and accept the sign of his native town, which is strange to him and frightens him. Józef runs away from it in search of another space where he wants to settle and build 'the republic of the young'. The energy of the Town wins (it is stronger because it is authentic) – and the narrator returns to the Town renouncing his dream. But the dream – 'the republic of dreams' – also returns and regenerates itself because nothing is wasted in Schulz's world. It has returned thanks to the Blue-eyed One who devoted himself to it, was faithful, and managed to subordinate individual creation to universal interpretation. The Blue-eyed One was a real interpreter who saved from oblivion and death the republic of dreams, which was a real, mystical, hidden and mysterious sense of the town.

In Schulz's 'project of creative work' the energy of creation and interpretation are combined and create the whole because only then they have their sense.

The Republic of Dreams: Town in Schulz's creation and interpretation

The story The Republic of Dreams *should be read as philosophical and poetical treatise about the art of interpretation. This work looks like a sonnet, perfectly organized, rhythmically and metaphorically finished but its synthesis poses new questions, creates the intrigue of Infinity where the end becomes the beginning. Schulz leaves one fundamental question without an answer: can everyone be a builder of 'the republic of dreams'?*

What is the meaning of Drohobycz in Schultz's writing? From various possible answers there will emerge Town as universe, which is everything in the creative work of the Artist: from the most important and the biggest things to minor, fragmentary, disappearing, and trivial elements. Town is for Schultz both a place where creation happens and the act of creation. In a sense, his work is an act of Town, a never ending text or meta text about Town, which does not fit on the pages of his poetic prose and transcends the written text.

Schultz act of Town will last eternally. This phenomenon is not the result of real determinants of Drohobycz and its history; it is not about contemporary Drohobycz or Drohobycz from the past, where Schultz lived. Mythologized, mystical, to a certain extend sacral infinity of Town is always authentic, even though it seems somewhat exaggerated, overgrown metaphorically-sublime yet, at times, anxious and entangled in vicissitudes. Despite all differences and unevenness in external and inner portrait of Town, for the creator of 'regions of great heresy', a seeker of its sense and value, a discoverer of a forgotten and lost reality, Town forever remains 'a mythological nest', the pretext of the actual text, the text itself, the beginning of creation and interpretation.

It is hard to find even one text in Schultz's literary output that would not be situated in Town, would not be provoked, and brought to life by Town. *Cinnamon Shops, Sanatorium under the Sign of the Hourglass,* other short stories, letters and essays, everything Schultz wrote is under the sign of Town.

I would like to concentrate on one text only, *The Republic of Dreams,* because it contains the most general and at the same time very particular elements, even axiom of Schultz's creation and interpretation of Town. The author thinks about Town as if it were a distant dream yet still alluring and dear since it is not fulfilled.

I will begin with a creative and interpretative description of Drohobycz in *The Republic of Dreams.* This description is well known but somehow not fully absorbed by Schultz's readers:

> A good way to the south, where the mapped land shifts-fallow from the sun, bronzed and singed by the glow of summer like a ripe pear - there it stretches like a cat in the sun, that chosen land, that peculiar province, the town unique in all the world. There is no point in speaking of this place to the profane - no point in explaining it is from that long tongue of rolling land over there lapping up breath for the countryside in the summer conflagrations, that boiling island of land facing south, that lone spur sticking up among swarthy Hungarian vineyards, that this one particle of earth detaches itself out of the collective landscape and, trampling alone down an untried path, attempts to be a world in itself. Sealed in a self-sufficient microcosm, that town and its countryside have boldly installed themselves at the very brink of eternity.[1]

'That chosen land', 'that peculiar province', 'the town unique in all the world' - those three descriptions bound together as an unbreakable whole, are not only beautifying words, the product of Schultz' flourishing imagination. They are categories of primary and infinite sense. They are categories of eternity since they speak expressively about this Town, which transcends dimensions of a small town. These words speak about the Town's mission (redeeming qualities), uniqueness (non-recurrence, strangeness), and exclusiveness (universality). This is above-the-ordinary Town and it belongs to eternity. Schultz explains (not to the profane!) this association:

> For that country submits utterly to heaven, holds heaven over itself in vaulted colours, variform, intricate with cloisters, triforia, stained-glass roses, windows opening onto eternity. Year after year that country grows up into the sky, merges with the dawn redness, turns angelic in the reflected light of the greater atmosphere.[2]

Schultz's creation of Town is ascending to heaven, is aspiring to be united with heaven in somewhat unexpected, even violent way:

---

1 B. Schulz, *The Republic of Dreams, in The Collected Works of Bruno Schultz*, ed. Jerzy Ficowski, Picador, London, 1998, p. 226.

2 ibid., p. 266.

> Above that thin forlorn snippet of land a sky deeper and broader than anywhere else, a sky like a vast gaping dome many storeys high, full of unfinished frescoes and improvisations, swirling draperies and violent ascensions, opens up once again.[3]

According to Christian theology, ascension of course cannot be violent. According to Schultz' axioms, it definitely can be violent. Indeed, it is a violent phenomenon when suddenly above this narrow and already lost piece of land the sky opens up one more time and the last time. This sky exists only here and it can provide ascension for an ordinary province. In the moment of Town's ascension, there is no need to further explain (even to the profane) this surprising subject of 'province of eternity' and 'the eternity of the province'.

Schultz's Town is nameless because it is eternal and it experienced ascension. Its earthly name does not weigh much. This Town is called now cosmos, infinity, and universe. Mortal Drohobycz transforms into immortal one. It keeps incarnating again and again until finally it turns into nameless cosmos:

> *Just beyond the toll gates the map of the region turns nameless and cosmic like Canaan.*[4]

Undoubtedly, the Biblical Canaan in *The Republic of Dreams* and generally in Schultz's creation and interpretation is the sign of 'that peculiar province', the key to its mark, uniqueness, and eternity. 'That peculiar province' is where Abraham started his journey; it is the Promised Land, which has to be conquered at a high price. Drohobycz, 'the town unique in all the world', becomes something different. It is not the gray and provincial Drohobycz but a hidden, secretive, eternal, and ascended town, the true Promised Land, towards which we should stride and for which we should fight like Canaanites did, despite Israelites cursing them and their cities, despite all obstacles on the way to the Promised Land. If 'that peculiar province' were prone to idolatry (Book of Judges 3, 5–6; Book of Ezra 9, 1–2).

One can be tempted to compare Schultz with a Biblical Canaanite who fights for his Promised Land, who creates for himself and the whole world

---

3 ibid., p. 266.
4 ibid., p. 266.

a different Drohobycz, unknown to others before and after him and who in this ascended town creates 'A Book of Idolatry', which dazzles the town and its inhabitants. For this Town is a land of love, which never disappears (as opposed to the Apollinaire's vision presented in *The song of Unloved* (1909)). How could eternity ever disappear?

Schultz describes 'that peculiar province', creates and interprets it at the same time, and then he poses a question: 'How to express this in words?' The province is the primal sense and its secret cannot be solved. Suddenly Schultz's superb language is not enough. Hence the question: 'How to express this in words?' It is difficult to express the sense of that peculiar province, because of the distance between this town 'unique in all the world', which 'regressed into essence' and other towns, which 'evolved into statistics'. In this province:

> Nothing happens here by chance, nothing results without deep motive and premeditation. Here events are not ephemeral surface phantoms; they have roots sunk into the deep of things and penetrate the essence. Here decisions take place every moment, laying down precedents once and for all. Everything that happens here happens only once and is irrevocable. This is why such weightiness, such heavy emphasis, such sadness inheres in what takes place.[5]

In this province nothing is on the surface, everything here reaches in depth of things; it reaches the essence of being. It is very important that each event happens here 'only once' but at the same time 'once and for all'. How to understand it and, what is more difficult, how to express it? It can be understood although not by everybody: the ascension happens only once and for all. In Schultz's province 'nothing happens by chance' because all is eternal. It is more difficult to express it as Schultz taught us in *The Mythologizing of Reality:*

> The essence of reality is Meaning or Sense. What lacks sense is, for us, not reality. Every fragment of reality lives by virtue of partaking in a universal sense… The nameless does not exists for us. To name something means to include it in some universal sense.[6]

5 ibid., p. 267.

6 ibid., p. 371.

Indeed, the biggest problems are with naming and expressing the reality. Someone who names the unnamed things carries a big responsibility of including unnamed in universal, eternal sense. Is Schultz afraid of this responsibility when he asks 'how to express it?' I am convinced he is not. The ability to name things was his destination more so than other artists' who ever lived in 'that peculiar province' known in history as Drohobycz. Schultz was not afraid, he was sad as any mortal would be at the thought that all that is important happens 'only once' for those who witness it. Events happen once also for Schultz - the discoverer, the brilliant interpreter, who in this situation is not a creator. He did not create this other, ascended town; he is only the interpreter of hidden primary sense, a deep and relevant meaning extending towards eternity.

The ascended town, which in Schultz's creation measures up to the exceptional land and miraculously balances 'on the verge of eternity', becomes consequential through small, seemingly insignificant, things. It is only an illusion because 'nothing happens here by chance, nothing results without deep motive and premeditation'. That is why weeds and nettles and crooked sheds, 'enormous bristly burdocks that grow right to the eves of the shingled roofs',[7] are signs of Town's Universe and attest to Town's Infinity. The deep sense of all that happens here once and for all materializes in town through the most trivial things:

> The town lives under the sign of the Weed, of wild, avid, fanatical plant life bursting out in cheap, coarse greenery-toxic, rank, parasitic. That greenery glows under the sun's conjury, the maws of the leaves suck in seething chlorophyll; armies of nettles, rampant, voracious, devour the flower plantings, break into the gardens, spread over the unguarded back walls of houses and barns overnight, run wild in the roadside ditches. It is amazing what insane vitality, feckless and unproductive, lives in this fervid dab of green, this distillate of sun and ground water.[8]

The Narrator is amazed at this 'insane vitality', he cannot recognize and interpret that 'fervid dab of green', which exists in spite of everything almost against

[7] ibid., p. 267.

[8] ibid., p. 267.

the intention of the Town which suddenly finds itself under the sign of the weed and cannot hide from own vitality, cannot keep the status of 'flower plantings' civilization. The Narrator deciphered and metaphorically expressed the sign of this voracious, insane vitality; he did not interpret and absorb it.

If 'an exemplary' event such as 'insane vitality' happens in Town, the interpretive power of the Narrator is consumed by the event; he is left only with his creative energy. As a consequence, the creator runs away deprived of his interpretive depth:

> What to do on those days, where to flee from the conflagration, from the incubus lying heavy on the chest in a torrid noontime nightmare?[9]

The Narrator runs away. Together with his family he goes to Little Hill. He cannot fully escape the Town; only its edges are receding. It is impossible to run away from all that happens only once and for all even if it is impossible to understand and accept it.

How the Town does behave when its resident runs away? How does it defend itself from the conflagration and nightmare? It falls asleep, enters the dead season. Or does it? 'Distant prospects' still 'lie in a dazzled faint in the heat-glazed sky', and give the Town peace and permanence despite being 'rumpled from the flight' and unconscious. In the moment of helplessness the Narrator claims the prospects are 'already spent'. He only thinks so because, blinded by the sun, exhausted by the heat of the weeds, he lets deep slumber crawl onto him. The prospects, however, are 'waiting for a new charge of brilliance, in which to renew themselves'. This glow will rise towards them from the eternal and indestructible energies of Town. Before it happens, Town chooses a different season but it is never a dead season.

'The sign of the weed' provokes a certain confrontation between Schultz's creation and interpretation of Town and as a divider it contrapositions the energy of creation and the energy of interpretation. The latter is more important for Schultz but more difficult to acquire, it is whimsical and fleeting, while the former is a gift Schultz received at the beginning, which will last forever. Under 'the sign of the weed', Town interprets itself pretending the dead season. The Narrator is saving himself by escaping and for a moment remains only the creator of his Town giving up on the effort of its interpretation.

---

9 ibid., p. 268.

The Narrator brilliantly created the destination and the climate of the escape. He planned to continue it, to extend it, and give it (he admits his ideas are absurd) a rather imaginary sense. Together with his friends he wanted to 'proclaim the Republic of the Young', 'into no man's or God's land', within 'borders both neutral and disputed'.[10] The Narrator leaves his Town and intends to go to a place that does not exist. He consciously creates absurd reality: running away from 'the sign of the weed', which he does not understand and is not able to accept in his own Town, he is looking for the sign of poetry and adventure in a place that does not exist. Moving away from the nature of a place destined for him, he seeks different, imagined nature, which will shower him with 'honeyed discourse of fables and novels, romances and epics'.[11] The farther away he moves in his creation from his place, the more ambitious are his plans to create a different place, which should be familiar but is foreign, which should compensate for all he was not able to discover, understand and accept in his Town. Those ambitions spring into slogans that pretend to be conceptual yet they lack sense and are not rooted in the essence of things. These slogans are 'self-sufficient', 'new life' and 'new era'. The ideal, 'the Republic of the Young' was supposed to be based on those slogans and function as a closed world, a fortress, 'a fortified base ruling the neighbourhood'. Why fortress? Because the plan for the new republic anticipated dangerous situations, unfortunately in no way specified thus unreal and insignificant.

The essence of being remained behind the walls of that not existing fortress. It stayed in front of the walls and above them, where the real town exists, a town developed not in widths as a fortress but upwards, up to the distant prospects. Anyone who leaves the real town is bound for failure. That is why the plan of the Republic of the Young could never be realized. The dreams of 'the Young' were in vain. They remained dreams and they are revisited:

> Today those remote dreams come back and not without reason. The possibiliy suggests itself that no dreams, however absurd or senseless, are wasted in the universe.[12]

Who will realize the dream that originated as an excellent plan of escaping the reality and, simultaneously, as a hunger for reality (again, it is a confrontation

10 ibid., p. 269.

11 ibid., p. 269.

12 ibid., p. 270.

of creative and interpretative energies of the dream's author)? It is not the one who designed it. The designer, willing or unwilling, returns to his reality. He returns to Town, which is stronger than he, overwhelms him energetically because from its beginnings it is a primary sense. The Town's resident returns and renounces the dream that somehow is not "wasted in the universe" and comes back not without a reason. The dream returns in a different shape, in different interpretation, in somebody else's interpretation. This person does not run away from his own world to chase the dream. He finds the dream, abandoned and unrealized, and embraces it as his own world - the fulfillment of his destiny.

This time, it is not the fugitive but the wanderer, the seeker, the discoverer who arrives in the neighbourhood of unfulfilled dream where he finds 'a sovereign realm of poetry'. He was searching for this realm, he was striding towards it. He was able to hear its call, did not intend to run from it as someone happened to do earlier. He was faithful and that is why he was chosen by the realm of poetry. He discovered a true sense without changing anything a small scale, to be sure, for us alone, but after our own tastes and pleasures.[13] He did it in accordance with the Highest Plan, which revealed itself in front of him:

> He discovered in the atmosphere the performed outlines of this concept, the planes, elevations, and stone tablets of data. He heard a summons, an inner voice, like Noah did when he received his orders and instructions.
>
> He was visited by the spirit of this design, which wandered at large in the atmosphere. He proclaimed a Republic of Dreams, a sovereign realm of poetry… He staked out its borders, laid down the foundations for a fortress, converted the realm into a single great rose garden.[14]

This was the work of the Blue-eyed One, who like Biblical Noah fulfilled God's Will by offering it, understanding, and interpreting. Interpretation wins over creation when someone is destined to fulfill something of the essence. The Blue-eyed One, a traveler, a person who is not invented (the narrator says: 'I

13 ibid., p. 269.

14 ibid., p. 271.

have seen this person, I have spoken with him'[15]) becomes a protagonist of a narrator who is a fugitive, a creator, and a dreamer. This traveler has the gift of effective interpretation.

We see here the results of the effectiveness, generosity and understanding: the abandoned and forgotten neighbourhoods of dreams are transformed into 'single great rose garden'. We are reminded of an inquisitive question posed by Józio from Gombrowicz's *Ferdydurke:* 'Whose neighbourhood is this?' No one was able to answer Józio, even Zosia's answer was deceitful. Schultz's Józef is in a different situation: after abandoning his neighbourhood, he never finds another real one. This is what he gets for momentarily giving up on sense intended for him. The Blue-eyed One on the other hand finds this imagined, lost, and nonexistent neighbourhood as his own, as the territory where he will fulfill something most significant, as he should, since the territory is 'a sign of poetry' given to him once and for all.

'The sign of poetry' becomes for the Blue-eyed One the only real sense he can find and be devoted to. For the narrator the sign of poetry was a mere fantasy, a substitute being, and the escape from the foreign 'sign of the Weed'.

The traveler discovered 'the republic of dreams'. He liberated it from oblivion, saved from annihilation. What is that 'republic of dreams' in regards to the abandoned Town? It is the same Town, its inner, hidden side, its secret never comprehended by the Town's dwellers. Józef also does not understand it. He believes he will be able to create an additional, illegal sense of Town, but that proves to be impossible, absurd, and empty. A renounced dream returns to Town and its residents as 'the sign of poetry' purposely hidden under 'the sign of the weed', giving the impression of emptiness, decay and lifelessness. The dream returns also to Józef, who gave up on it and stopped believing.

The Blue-eyed One saves the 'republic of dreams' by devotedly fulfilling his mission. He is Messiah who left his worldly life, 'town and matters', 'days and their fever' in order to 'hear a summons' and fulfill it. By doing so he liberated himself from everything that is insignificant, material, earthy: without creating anything in his own way as his predecessors tried to do, to reconstitute the world-on?

> He has entered a radiant new holiday regularity, has cast off his own body like a bony carapace, has shed a grimacing

[15] ibid., p. 271.

> mask that had grown onto his face, has completed the liberating metamorphosis.[16]

The Blue-eyed One Messiah was the most brilliant interpreter. We have no doubt about it and even Schultz suggests: 'The man with the sky–blue eyes is no architect. He is, rather, a director'.[17] Then he explains, what he means by using metaphorical forms of a philosophical treatise about the art of interpretation:

> He is, rather, a director, a director of cosmic landscapes and sceneries. His art consists in catching nature's intentions in midair, knowing how to read her arcane ambitions. For nature is full of potential architecture, rife with plans and constructions. Did the master builders of the great ages behave any differently? They eavesdropped on the immense pathos of squares, the dynamic perspectives of distance, the silent pantomime of symmetrical lanes.[18]

The Blue-eyed One was not an architect; he did not build 'the republic of dreams; it always existed; it was built at the very beginning. Of course, it was not built by Józef, who strived to be its new architect, wanted to create it accordingly to his own specifications. This was an insignificant substitute of creativity. The Blue-eyed One is a director, the interpreter of 'potential architecture'. He understands primary intentions of nature, can discover the secret of the world and through individual, lonely acts of discovery and interpretation, he is able to reveal for others this dazzling secret by offering them his Messianic gift and through this offer he can liberate himself from his human limitations.

According to Schultz, the director-interpreter liberates himself from his ego and is ready to decipher the primary sense he did not know existed. Because it exists it requires a tremendous will to understand its intentions, its deeply hidden potential. The director discovers not only what he intends to discover, is not only looking for what he wishes to find; he is not only looking for himself reflected in primordiality. The Blue-eyed One is a director and not an architect because he decides to relate to the other, the unknown, the unsettling; and by doing so he challenges himself with the most difficult task in the art of

16 ibid., p. 271.
17 ibid., p. 271.
18 ibid., p. 271.

interpretation. Schultz's reflections are even today one of the clearest requirements in the art of interpretation: the interpreter should discover in a text not only the meaning he invested in it earlier. Janusz Sławiński is convinced that:

> You need to know that your interpretation is from the beginning bound for inaccuracy; don't have any illusions that you will be able to interpret the text in a way that could have been binding for anybody else, that you will find an objective, "relevant" key to its meanings; you will discover in a text only what you have invested in it, which is your own interpretation.[19]

It does not mean, however, that the interpreter's individual creative expectations will not be fulfilled, when he will choose to sacrifice the universal sense, which is still intriguing in its infiniteness. These expectations are fulfilled through the interpretive energy and faithfulness to the interpretation. This is when the creative energy achieves the desired results.

Let us return one more time to Schultz's phrases describing interpretation as 'catching nature's intentions', 'knowing how to read her arcane ambitions', 'eavesdropping on the immense pathos of great squares, the dynamic perspectives of distance, the silent pantomime of symmetrical lanes'. They seem to be a metaphorical paraphrase of theoretical explanation of relations between text's intentionalism and author's intentions, which are in a way a secondary creative energy in relation to the overwhelming energy of text. Schultz, who is simultaneously a creator and an interpreter of sense, calls into being the Text, which, according to Roman Ingarden,[20] would be kept alive by the reader.

The Text with its intentionality exists inside and outside of the relation to the author. The author is first and foremost a person who received this intentionality, in front of whom the text reveals itself and invites to be interpreted. Through interpreting this meta-text of the world, of nature, of 'the potential architecture', the primary 'designing and building', the author realizes his intentions, fulfills his personal intention as a creator, at the same time overcomes

19 Janusz Sławiński, *Próby teoretycznoliterackie. Prace wybrane,* vol IV, Universitas, Kraków 2000, p. 60

20 Zofia Majewska, *Świat kultury Romana Ingardena,* Wydawnistwo Uniwersytetu Marii Curie-Skłodowskiej, Lublin, 2001

the limitations of individual creation. It is easy to understand Schultz's demand for a necessary hierarchy in constructing ways of interpretation and creation which, when united, achieves the highest harmony, 'an architecture of grandiose inspiration, an ethereal transcendental brand of urbanistics'.[21]

The Blue-eyed One - the Messiah - who is awaited by the inhabitants of Schultz's Town, is an ideal example of blending the interpreter and the creator in one person. What is left for Józef? He is aware of how exceptional was his encounter and the conversation with the Blue-eyed One. Let us add: if they talked, then Józef had to learn, if he learned, then he had a chance to comprehend. Did he indeed comprehend? Did he realize why he had to return to the Town and why, against all odds, 'the republic of dreams' was saved? Why the dream 'hanging above the neighbourhood' also did return to the Town? We do not have an answer to those questions. All we know is that there has always been a fundamental difference between human creation and a creation of someone who in the act of creation goes beyond limits of his own creativity, does not lock himself in it as sometimes humans do lock themselves in realities they created for themselves to their utmost satisfaction. Schultz concludes *The Republic of Dreams:*

> Human works have the peculiarity that, once completed, they become hermetic, cut off from nature, consolidated on a base of their own. The work of the Blue-eyed One, in contrast, has not cut itself off from the great cosmic contexts; it is immersed in them half-humanized like a centaur, harnessed to the sublime processes of nature, still unfinished and growing. The man with the sky-blue eyes invites everyone to keep on working, fabricating, jointly creating: we are all of us dreamers by nature, after all, brothers under the sign of the trowel, destined to be master builders.[22]

It is easy to fall in an unexpected trap prepared by Schultz for all those who are still not ready for this conclusion. This is Schultz's famous intrigue of Infinity discovered, explained and mystified by Władysław Panas, which makes us return again and again to the beginning. Was Józef, the wonderful dreamer, excellent builder and creator finally justified? Yes and no.

21 B. Schulz, The Republic.... op.cit., p. 272.

22 ibid., p. 272

He was justified because he already spoke with the Blue-eyed One and in a sense became the continuator of his work unique and different from all other human works.

He was not justified because he did not overcome himself and kept looking for the sense he could understand, ran away from what was incomprehensible, disquieting, threatening to his stability, which was based on 'his own rules'. Those rules will prove correct in *Sanatorium under the Sign of the Hourglass* where he escapes again, this time from his father because he cannot comprehend the different existence in the Sanatorium. He runs from the Town, which seems foreign to him, which shows him a different face and exists in different aura, even though it is still his home town. Józef runs away when he feels helpless as an interpreter and when his creation cannot sustain him.

The last sentence in *The Republic of Dreams* is not the end. Again, it is a scheme that seduces, inspires, deludes us that our nature of dreamers and builders is the most important for us; that we are all invited by the Blue-eyed One to design and build. There is more. The Blue-eyed One's opus is different from all our works, finished or unfinished, it 'has not cut itself off from the great cosmic contexts', because its Author was not an architect, he was a director. No doubt, he was also a builder. What kind of a builder was he? Who designed the project? Why he was not confined to its boundaries? Schultz returns to those questions, does not answer them, starts again his treatise about 'the republic of dreams' and has no intention to finish it. Schultz's (not Józef's or the Blue-eyed One's) 'republic of dreams' becomes the work of Infinity and is also a part of 'great cosmic contexts'.

It is easy to convince someone that *The Republic of Dreams* is a classical philosophical treatise about Town, about searching and finding 'the republic of dreams', which nevertheless remains a dream, an unfinished work that belongs to Infinity. The evidence is easy to find in the text.

I am tempted to call *The Republic of Dreams* a sonnet, not necessarily in the Shakespeare or Petrarch style but an intricate poetic form in a particular style of philosophical discourse where there are rules about the relation between subject and a reflection on subject, or among thesis, antithesis and synthesis. The sonnet is three - dimensional and its homogeneity and harmony are indeed fascinating. 'The town unique in all the world', 'that peculiar province', 'that chosen land', - all that is an overwhelming subject of Town, which in *The Republic of Dreams* acquires categorical dimension. This subject, in the first part of the text, is an axiom accepted in whole as a dogma, becomes at the same time a philosophical thesis, which allows its own contradiction.

The narrator, the subject of the act of Town, is the contradiction. He does not understand a certain sign that endangers his safety in the Town; he looks for a substitute sign, which ruins the primary order and harmony of previously shaped reception of Town. It never ruins though the infinite values and senses of Town. The Blue-eyed One appears and he, not Schultz or the narrator, formulates thoughts and takes actions that save 'the republic of dreams' and gives back to the Town its categorical stability.

The subject changes in Schultz's sonnet. This is the most surprising. The subject's (i.e. the Blue-eyed One's) action and work are in a sense final but the subject matter and Józef somehow return to the starting point. There is no solution the sonnet had a clear conclusion but it cannot satisfy anyone, who is still not certain if there is enough of a dreamer and builder in him in order to understand the Town and stay in it forever.

It is uncertain if there is enough human activity to allow the inhabitants to stay in the Town forever, to be faithful and kind to the Town. This uncertainty is an attribute and the value of Schultz's creation and interpretation of Town.

Bruno Schultz stayed in his Town for better and for worse, he was not looking for the substitute signs, he stayed until the end, which again and again becomes the beginning. The author of *The Republic of Dreams* made a choice and that is why he himself was chosen. Władysław Panas comments on the tensions and returns of the end and the beginning, which encompass life, work, and the reception of Schultz's literary work:

> ...the beginning points to the end, but the end is somehow a symbolic return to the beginning. In Schultz's life and death the plot of Infinity drew a surprising circle: he was killed, as we know, at Czackiego Street (today Szewczenki Street), not far from a house, where he was born, which stood at the market's corner. This is one circle. The other confines Schultz's writing and also binds together the beginning and the end, the end and the beginning. Infinity prepared an unexpected surprise also in that sphere.[23]

Translated from Polish by Anna Wróbel

[23] Władysław Panas, *Willa Bianki. Mały przewodnik drohobycki dla przyjaciół* (fragments), ed. Paweł Próchniak, Wydawnictwo Uniwersytetu Marii Curie-Skłodowskiej, Lublin, 2006, p. 10.

Lectures de l'œuvre plastique de Bruno Schulz

Maria Poprzęcka - Université de Varsovie

Resumé

L'œuvre de Schulz « grandit dans et sur des contradictions et elle se nourrit de contradictions ». Le principe même d'analyser le travail de cet artiste est déjà sujet à controverses, pour la bonne raison que nous n'en possédons qu'une infime partie. À cette affirmation, chargée de tant d'incertitudes et de doutes, qu'étant donné que nous ne connaissons pas tout Schulz, écrire sur lui est une « activité à hauts risques », on peut opposer cette autre affirmation, qui porte le poids d'une conviction très forte, « qu'au corpus des textes connus de Schulz l'on peut tout autant ajouter de nouveaux textes que l'on peut les omettre : le dessin qu'ils contiennent de la totalité de la vision du monde reste assez imperméable à ce genre d'opération ». Cependant son œuvre plastique nous offre-t-elle et nous livre-t-elle une « vision totale et totalisante » ? L'analyse de cette œuvre ne serait-elle pas que l'ébauche de la reconstruction d'un tableau à partir de quelques « debris de miroir »? Et puis quelle est la relation entre son œuvre littéraire et son œuvre plastique ? Pour ce qui est de mon intervention elle se résumera en une tentative de mettre à jour les controverses et questionnements que soulève cette dernière.

Les œuvres plastiques de Bruno Schulz que nous connaissons, jusqu'à ce jour, comportent : un tableau à l'huile, 26 gravures réalisées au moyen d'une technique rare *clichés-verre*, quelques centaines de dessins, un petit nombre de projets graphiques à but utilitaire[1], des fragments de peintures murales de la villa occupée par le SS Landau à Drohobycz. L'on sait que cette liste n'est pas complète d'où les recherches qui durent et la croyance inaltérable de découvrir d'autres pièces dûes à la main de cet artiste. L'arrivée sur le marché des antiquités d'un tableau à l'huile (1992) ainsi que, il n'y a pas si longtemps de cela (2001), la découverte d'une fresque dans la villa de Landau - découverte qui a fait du bruit et s'est trouvée entourée d'une aura de scandale[2] – ont réveillé de nouvelles espérances dans l'apparition de nouvelles œuvres perdues ou cachées, ce qui peut et pourra paradoxalement entraîner la démultiplication de faux.

[1] Wojciech Chmurzyński, *Bruno Schulz 1892–1942. Rysunki i archiwalia ze zbiorów Muzeum Literatury im. A. Mickiewicza w Warszawie,* Muzeum Literatury im. A. Mickiewicza, Warszawa 1992.
[2] W. Budzyński, *Wyprawa po Schulza* dans catalogue de l'exposition *Bruno Schulz. Republika marzeń,* Muzeum Literatury im. A. Mickiewicza, Warszawa, 2003, p. 159–168.

L'intérêt critique et scientifique de l'œuvre plastique de Schulz, bien que tangible, ne peut être comparé à celui que l'on porte à son œuvre littéraire. Schulz – peintre et dessinateur, au contraire de Schulz – prosateur, ne possède pas comme ce dernier ses quelques générations d'exégètes. Aucune « lecture » de son œuvre n'est jusqu'à aujourd'hui apparue comme dominante et des plus suggestives. L'on peut plutôt parler dans son cas de variations interprétatives et moins de polémiques. Cette disproportion d'intérêts des chercheurs est-elle le reflet de la disproportion existante entre l'œuvre littéraire et l'œuvre plastique, ou est-elle le résultat de difficultés méthodologiques, qui surgissent toujours lorsque l'on analyse des œuvres provenant de domaines artistiques hétérogènes, et des relations réciproques entre le mot et l'image ?

L'œuvre plastique de Schulz est le plus souvent appréhendée sous la forme de deux contextes bien différents : le premier relève de la psychobiographie et le deuxième se rapporte à son œuvre littéraire en tant que telle. Du reste, le caractère autobiographique de l'œuvre de Schulz provoque par la force des choses que ces deux contextes sont bien souvent inséparables. La tendance biographique est renforcée également par la présence dans cette œuvre de Drohobycz et de sa réalité qui a été scrupuleusement identifiée et analysée par les chercheurs. « Toute l'œuvre de Schulz peut être vue comme une sorte d'autoportrait » conclut le plus fervent d'entre eux , Jerzy Ficowski[3].

Dans les œuvres plastiques la présence de cet autoportrait est évidente. Les hommes avilis dans *Le livre idolâtre,* le jeune juif orthodoxe dans le tableau à l'huile *La Rencontre,* les héros des illustrations des romans, de nombreux personnages masculins des dessins, que cela soit les clients assis à des tables en compagnie de femmes nues, ou le passant timide regardant humblement les cocottes se promenant à travers les rues portent tous les traits de l'artiste. En tant qu' « autoportrait d'un masochiste et d'un fétichiste qui s'affiche en pleine lumière »[4] voilà comment est vu avant tout *Le livre idolâtre.* La plus importante des œuvres plastiques de Schulz, ceci ne fait aucun doute, a vu le jour au début des années 20, et donc à l'époque « pré-littéraire, autonome et non illustratrice ». C'est elle aussi qui éveille le plus de controverses parmi les commentateurs. Les parentés artistiques sont ici évidentes et ne prêtent pas à discussion. C'est moins tant les « démonologues », auxquels faisait référence

[3] J. Ficowski, *Portraits et autoportraits* dans cataloque de l'exposition *Bruno Schulz. La république des rêves,* Musée d'art et d'histoire du Judaisme, Paris 2004, p. 75.

[4] S. Barańczak, „Twarz Brunona Schulza" dans *Bruno Schulz in memoriam,* red. M. Kitowska-Łysiak, Fis, Lublin 1994, p. 28.

Witkacy[5] que Goya ainsi et avant tout les décadents « satanistes » et mysogynes – Rops, von Stuck, Beardsley, Kubin[6]. Si *Le Livre* éveillent l'intérêt, il soulève aussi simultanément chez le lecteur l'embarras et la gêne, moins par le caractère « indécent »[7] de son graphisme que par son exhibitionnisme; l'exhibitionnisme qui s'exprime par l'intermédaire de ses femmes avilis, de ses hommes humiliés et battus ayant pour visage celui de l'artiste lui-même. « Schulz se découvre [ici] beaucoup plus que dans sa prose. D'où le contact avec son œuvre qui nous embarrasse et nous gêne. Elle rappelle une confession que l'on voudrait ne pas entendre »[8].

La discussion sur cette œuvre tourne donc autour de cette question : *Le livre idolâtre* a-t-il un caractère purement confessionnel ? Est-il la mise à jour de tendances sexuelles des plus intimes ou ne reflète-il que les thèmes d'une époque bien déterminée ? Longtemps « l'axiome de la schulzologie »[9] n'aura été que ce que Witkacy en avait dit : « le sadisme des femmes lié avec le masochisme des hommes ».

Cette lecture masochiste fut propagée par Artur Sandauer, critique, qui avait personnellement connu Schulz et qui après la guerre fit beaucoup pour le faire non seulement connaître mais aussi reconnaître. Sandauer est allé jusqu'à affirmer que le masochisme de Schulz dominait sa personnalité et qu'en atteignant les limites de l'autodestruction il fut la cause de sa fin tragique (l'écrivain hésitait à s'enfuir du ghetto de Drohobycz ayant pourtant avec lui des « papiers aryens » etc.)[10]. D'un autre côté Sandauer souligne également, ce qui est le fait du pur hasard, que Leopold von Sacher-Masoch était de Lvov, non loin de Drohobycz, capitale de la Galicie, et que par conséquent « ce qui parfois est

[5] S. I. Witkiewicz, *Wywiad z Brunonem Schulzem* [1935] dans S. I. Witkiewicz, *Bez kompromisu. Pisma krytyczne i publicystyczne,* red. J. Degler, Państwowy Instytut Wydawniczy, Warszawa 1976, p. 181.

[6] Je laisse de côtés ici les qualifications les plus primaires de l'œuvre de Schulz que constituent toutes les tentatives de l'inclure sous différents -ismes : l'expressionnisme, le formisme, et même le surréalisme. Cela ne va pas ici sans présupposé (par exemple : Schulz « a pu voir » du Schiele, Witkacy « a pu voir » du Chagall et en parler à Schulz etc.).

[7] Exposé dans une galerie très académique Zachęta.

[8] E. Kuryluk, „Gąsienicowy pojazd, czyli podróż Brunona Schulza w przyszłość przeszłości" dans *Bruno Schulz in memoriam,* op. cit., p. 233.

[9] W. Bolecki, „Witkacy – Schulz, Schulz – Witkacy" dans *Czytanie Schulza,* red. J. Jarzębski, Oficyna naukowa i literacka, Kraków, 1994, p. 128.

[10] A. Sandauer, „Rzeczywistość zdegradowana (Rzecz o Brunonie Schulzu)" dans *Zebrane pisma krytyczne. Studia o literaturze współczesnej,* Warszawa, 1981, pp. 557–580.

appelé *le vice anglais* peut être défini d'une façon des plus pertinentes sous le nom du symptôme galicien»[11]. «La version standard de la légende de l'artiste fait que son visage a les traits inaltérables de la grimace d'un masochiste»[12] conclut Stanisław Barańczak. Il ne fait aucun doute que c'est bien son œuvre plastique qui est à l'origine de cette légende et qui a créé ce portrait de l'artiste, surtout *Le livre idolâtre,* et pas sa prose, dont le motif de l'humiliation n'apparaît jamais sous une forme si insistante et si littéralement sexuelle.

Les révisions de cette image d'un Schulz masochiste s'appuient sur différents types d'argumentation. Ainsi les gravures du *Livre idolâtre* sont «une réinterprétation spécifique du motif moderniste de la *femme fatale*»[13], une démythification ironique de «la femme démoniaque»[14], et «d'une relation paradoxale à l'avant-garde»[15] et non l'expression de complexes étouffés et cachés, mais «un jeu avec un contexte» bien précis[16]. Ce contexte, dont il est question ici, c'est cet ensemble de représentations de la «femme fatale» typiques du modernisme qui régnait à la charnière du XIXème et XXème siècle : perverse, jeune adolescente androgyne, *La belle dame sans merci* dans le plein épanouissement de sa féminité, femme mante religieuse ou vampire. L'autre partie indispensable pour que ce répertoire soit complet ce sont les victimes du sadisme féminin en la personne d'hommes humiliés, et ce de différentes façons, ainsi que toute une panoplie d'accesoires : des lits richement ornés, des cravaches et naturellement le fétiche masochiste par excellence : les pantoufles pour dames. Le conventionnalisme de ces représentations, vues dans un contexte érotique, souvent celui de l'art pervers *fin-de-siècle* est incontestable. Peut-on cependant estimer que Schulz, créant son premier et si important travail, conscient et plein de distance, a joué avec ces conventions, ou n'était-il pas plutôt profondément immergé en elles après séjours, récents, dans la Vienne d'alors? Pouvait-il ironiser? Nous nous souvenons que Witkacy déjà

11 B. Budurowycz, „Galicja w twórczości Bruno Schulza" dans *Bruno Schulz in memoriam*, op. cit., p. 15.

12 S. Barańczak, op. cit., p. 30.

13 I. Kossowska, „Odwieczna baśń" dans cataloque de l'exposition *Bruno Schulc, Republika marzeń*, op. cit., p. 137.

14 K. Kulik-Janarek, „Erotyka-groteska-ironia" dans *Bruno Schulz in memoriam*, op. cit., p. 153-174.

15 I., Ł. Kossowscy, „Właśnie: humor Schulza" dans *Wystawa ze zbiorów Muzeum Literatury im. A. Mickiewicza w Warszawie*, Wydawnictwo Uniwersytetu Marii Curie-Skłodowskiej, Lublin 2002, p. 30.

16 W. Bolecki, op. cit., p. 130.

en appelant *Le livre idolâtre* des « poèmes de jambes cruelles » désarmait et dévoilait à la fois leur « horrible pathos » en assurant que « ces jambes-ci sont récurées deux fois par jour et non pas de cors »[17]. Peut-on cependant attribuer à Schulz la raillerie Witkacéenne au sujet de « la métaphysique du sexe »? Ce jeune professeur de dessin de province, inconnu de tous, grattant inlassablement ses fantaisies érotiques sur des plaques de verre aurait-il pu se permettre à l'époque une quelconque « distance intellectuelle »[18] ? Distance, ironie, démarcation entre le sexe et l'art apparaissent effectivement bien, mais dans des déclarations de l'artiste beaucoup plus tardives, parfois même plusieurs années après (l'exemple le plus souvent cité et analysé est la lettre à Gombrowicz sur les belles cuisses de la « doctoresse de rue Wilcza »[19]. On peut donc se demander si l'auto-ironie était dès l'origine inscrite à la source de l'œuvre ou si elle est apparue au fur et à mesure des années et par l'obtention d'une certaine position dans le monde littéraire et dans le monde tout court. Enfin l'impertinente déclaration « macho » de la lettre à Gombrowicz : « C'est nous qui sommes la biologie guerroyante, la biologie du prédateur, nous qui sommes vraiment vitaux » peut-elle effacer « la grimace masochiste » de la représentation stéréotypée de Schulz, sur laquelle repose non seulement la déviance sexuelle dans *Le livre idolâtre,* mais aussi toute sa biographie ? Teodosia S. Robertson, en signalant, dans les déclarations de Schulz, rarement prises en compte, les éléments traditionnels de la comédie dramatique, fait remarqué que « la connaissance du destin tragique de Schulz pèse visiblement sur la façon de comprendre ses déclarations. Il se peut que les critiques se rapportent trop facilement dans leurs commentaires à la solitude, l'angoisse de l'artiste et son sentiment de demeurer un étranger »[20]. La fin tragique de Schulz influe également sur la vision que l'on a de son œuvre plastique, elle la dramatise, et y ajoute une tonalité eschatologique. C'est une vision qui dans l'histoire de l'art est actuellement définie comme « pré-postériorité » (preposterous history) – la connaissance des choses postérieures influe sur l'appréhension que l'on a des choses antérieures[21]. Mais voilà qu'ici même une question

[17] S. I. Witkiewicz, op. cit., p. 182.

[18] I., Ł. Kossowscy, op. cit., p. 24.

[19] S. Barańczak, op. cit., p. 37.

[20] T. Robertson, „Bruno Schulz i komedia" dans *Bruno Schulz in memoriam*, op.cit., p. 108.

[21] Le terme introduit par Mieke Bal *Quoting Caravaggio : Contemporary Art, Preposterous History,* University of Chicago Press, Chicago, London, 1999. Comme « pré-postériorité » l'on peut définir la réception de Schulz par des œuvres postérieures, telles que celles de Balthus, Pierre Klossowski, Bellmer, Jan Lebenstein. Naturellement ce n'est pas Schulz qui

s'impose et se pose : Des interprétations autres que psychologiques sont-elles possibles[22] ? Tout porte à croire que dans le cas de Schulz il n'est aucunement possible de séparer l'œuvre de son auteur. Il faut ici ajouter un autre problème qui apparaît dans la perspective biographique – l'origine juive de Schulz et, ce qui va avec, la tentative d'interpréter la totalité de son œuvre par le primat de la tradition cabalistique et messiannique[23].

Les recherches sur son œuvre sont condamnées au biographisme et, ce qui va de pair, à « l'interprétation de son œuvre par sa vie »[24]. Dans ce contexte on ne peut que s'étonner que l'œuvre de Schulz n'ait pas attendu jusqu'à ce jour des études plus sérieuses du côté de la psychanalyse ni de l'histoire de l'art représentée par le courant féministe[25].

Des arguments contre une lecture unilatérale du *Livre idolâtre* en tant que confession masochiste peuvent cependant résulter non pas tant de la biographie de l'artiste que de l'analyse des seuls moyens d'expression artistique. Et c'est ainsi qu'en tant que facteur nivelant et affaiblissant le caractère exhibitionniste des représentations imaginaires surgissent en et par elles des éléments grotesques ; c'est d'ailleurs ce grotesque qui doit alléger la tension obsessionnelle et déviante de ses dessins. Pour cette interprétation il semble cependant que l'important réside moins dans la découverte de moyens bien caractéristiques pour une esthétiques plastique du grotesque, comme par exemple la disproportion, mais bien plutôt dans la véritable pensée schulzienne du grotesque. Elle s'exprime non par une déformation qui ne toucherait que la surface des choses, mais bien au contraire par une déformation qui réside au cœur même de la perception du monde[26].

anticipe les artistes qui viennent après lui, mais c'est nous qui percevons son œuvre au travers de leurs œuvres.

22 W. Bolecki, op. cit., p. 137.

23 W. Panas, "Mesjasz rośnie pomału..." dans *Bruno Schulz in memoriam*, op. cit., p. 116.

24 W. Stróżewski, „O wielkości" dans *Rocznik Międzynarodowego Centrum Kultury, nr 3*, Kraków, 1994, p. 70.

25 Le caractère antiféministe de la prose de Schulz a été signalé par plusieurs chercheurs, entre autres Bolecki, op. cit, p. 130 ; S. Chwin, „Grzeszne manipulacje" dans *Czytanie Schulza*, op. cit p. 252. Je ne compte pas les articles écrits du point de vue de la critique littéraire d'Artur Sandauer dans les analyses psychanalytiques. À part ça l'on trouve des affirmations d'ordre général, du type : « Les dessins de Schulz sont apparus presque en même temps que les théories de Freud que l'artiste approuvait totalement. On peut donc affirmer qu'ils ne sont que des transpositions plastiques des conceptions du savant viennois» - W. Chmurzyński, *Schulziana w zbiorach Muzeum Literatury w Warszawie. Kształtowanie kolekcji i próba*

Un argument semblable contre le soi-disant caractère purement exhibitionniste et personnel des 'idolâtries' imaginaires crées par Schulz est celui qui insiste sur leur théâtralisation, leur conventionnalisme scénique. En effet, dans le *Livre* les images sont mises en scène comme des spectacles. Les arrangements se répètent. Nous sommes comme les témoins de répétitions théâtrales, perpétuellement renouvelées. C'est un théâtre traditionnel ou les acteurs ont des rôles, des gestes et des costumes bien définis[27].

Et enfin tombe la question : le thème de l'adoration dans *Le livre idolâtre* est-il seulement *Das Ewig Weibliche,* ou est-il aussi le *Livre* en tant que tel, y compris ses nombreuses références mythologiques et bibliques? « C'est un Apocryphe privé et confessionnel qu'il faut lire en y cherchant des clés dans au moins quelques codes culturels »[28] affirme Małgorzata Kitkowska-Łysiak, en remarquant dans l'œuvre de Schulz des significations non seulement strictement privées, mais également universelles. À la suite de cette proposition en arrive une autre celle de « lire entre les lignes » le *Livre* et de le lire en dehors du conflit des éléments du féminin et du masculin, « pour saisir les luttes archétypales des dualismes qui la constituent : Jour et Nuit, Ciel et Terre, Bien et Mal, Soleil et Lune, c'est l'anti-thèse Cosmos-Chaos, intérieur-extérieur, art-réalité, sacrum-profanum, et même vie-mort…[29]. Dans l'érotisme du Livre on a vu aussi une métaphore artistique : « 'L'hommage à la femme devient la métaphore de l'acte de création de l'œuvre d'art, qui ne peut exister sans sa dimension purement physique »[30].

Ne prétendant pas ici engager une discussion avec toutes les interprétations établies, on ne peut que retirer l'impression que c'est le satut artistique de Schulz-écrivain qui ne permet pas aux chercheurs de se contenter de ne

charakterystyki dzieł plastycznych [dans] *catalogue de l'exposition Bruno Schulz 1892–1942* op. cit, p. 10. Très décevante est la tentative d'appréhender la personnalité de Schulz au moyen de la psychiatrie : M. Tyszkiewicz, „O niektórych cechach osobowości Bruno Schulza" dans *Teatr pamięci Brunona Schulza,* op. cit., p. 80.

26 M. Kitowska-Łysiak, „Galicyjskie Caprichos" dans *Mowa i moc obrazów. Prace dedykowane profesor Marii Poprzęckiej,* Wydawnistwa Uniwersytetu Warszawskiego, Warszawa 2005, p. 71.

27 I. Kossowska, op. cit., p. 138; M. Kitowska-Łysiak, „Prywatny Apokryf. Czy Xięga (Bałwochwalcza) jest Księgą?" dans cataloque de l'exposition Republika marzeń, op. cit., p. 71.

28 M. Kitowska-Łysiak, „Prywatny Apokryf", ibid.

29 M. Kitowska-Łysiak, „Bruno Schulz – Xięga Bałwochwalcza : wizja-forma-analogia" dans *Bruno Schulz in memoriam,* op. cit., p. 149.

30 I. Kossowska, *Odwieczna baśń* dans cataloque de l' exposition *Republika marzeń,* op. cit., p. 141.

voir dans ses gravures que des représentions érotiques conventionnelles, ayant poussé sur le terreau d'obsessions misogynes, cas typique du décadentisme. Ici, nous arrivons au problème de la « lecture » de l'œuvre plastique de Schulz non pas à l'aide de sa biographie, mais au moyen de son œuvre littéraire. S'appuyer sur la prose Schulzienne en tant qu'opposition au contenu de ses représentations est un moyen accepté par tous les commentateurs, hormis quelques-uns.

Cependant quelques divergences se dessinent également ici. Premièrement : l'œuvre plastique de Schulz est-elle autonome ou partie « intégrante », 'inséparable', de son œuvre littéraire ? Ce sont les historiens d'art qui sont le plus du côté de « l'intégralité »[31], les critiques et historiens de la littérature sont enclins à en faire peu de cas[32]. La citation d'une lettre de Schulz à Witkacy souvent mise en avant montre que lui-même sur cette question avait des doutes : « À la question, si dans mes dessins apparaît le même motif que dans ma prose, je répondrais par l'affirmative. C'est la même réalité, seulement elle est découpée tout autrement. Le matériau, la technique agissent ici comme le principe de sélection. Le dessin délimite à ce matériau des frontières autres que celles de la prose. Voilà pourquoi il me semble que dans ma prose je me suis exprimé plus pleinement »[33]. Nous sommes ici en face du vieux problèmes de la *correspondance des arts* et devant les polémiques jamais éteintes entre les défenseurs de l'autonomie et ceux qui défendent l'hétéronomie des différents domaines artistiques et de leurs propres moyens d'expression. Bruno Schulz constitue par lui-même et en lui-même un cas particulier (bien qu'à l'époque pas si rare que ça) de l'écrivain-dessinateur, en cela illustrateur de ses propres œuvres littéraires. Rappelons que les théoriciens classiques de la littérature, René Wellek et Austin Warren, ont démontré l'impossibilité de passer d'un art à un autre, en s'appuyant justement sur des exemples de peintres écrivant et d'écrivains peignant[34]. Witkacy, à qui Schulz adressait ses doutes, affrimait « qu'écrire et peindre sont deux genres de création contraires que je n'ai pas été à même d'accoupler »[35].

31 W. Chmurzyński, *Schulziana* w zbiorach Muzeum Literatury w Warszawie, op. cit. pp. 7-18.

32 J. Jarzębski, *Brunona Schulza malowanie słowem* dans *Bruno Schulz in memoriam*, op. cit., p. 43.

33 B. Schulz, *Lettre de Schulz à S. I. Witkiewicz* [1935], cit. d'après, *Opowiadania. Wybór esejów i listów*, op. cit., p. 443-444.

34 R. Wellek, A. Warren, *Literary Theory, Criticism and History*, Sewanee Review, 68, 1960, p. 1-19.

35 S. I. Witkiewicz, *Listy niemieckie Witkacego do Romana i Stefanii Jaworskich,* trad. S. Jaworska, Twórczość, nr 10, 1959.

Au niveau thématique l'œuvre de Schulz peut paraître homogène ne fût-ce qu'en raison du caractère illustratif de beaucoup de ses dessins. L'image de ses représentations comme « une même réalité », mise en images et décrite seulement par des moyens différents, est renforcée par les expositions, les albums, les catalogues, qui lui sont consacrée et dans lesquels les textes tirés des œuvres en prose accompagnent les dessins et les gravures. Cette méthode largement répandue et admise dans la recherche d'une correspondance thématique, et dans la mise en place, parfois effectivement très proches de parallèles image-mot peut donner l'impression que la création de Schulz est un exemple idéal « de l'éclairage réciproque entre les arts ». Le tableau à l'huile *La Rencontre* a obtenu presque son équivalent littéraire par un collage de citations[36]. Et pourtant la confrontation des dessins et des textes qui leur correspondent expose d'une façon pénétrante « les frontières plus étroites » du médium visuel. Même les propres illustrations de Schulz pour ses romans montre leur insuffisance. Il suffit ici de quelques exemples : la ville, l'un des plus importants motifs, le plus mythique de la prose de Schulz, est dans les dessins réduite à des maisons en miniatures et faites de cubes, ne ressemblant à rien d'autre qu'à une misérable scénographie d'un théâtre ambulant pouvant servir de toile de fond à n'importe quel spectacle. Dans les dessins, même ceux qui sont illustratifs, la nature, les arbres, les fleurs, les plantes brillent par leur absence, alors que dans sa prose elle est très présente. Nous ne rappelerons ici que les célèbres descriptions schulziennes des mauvaises herbes poussant dans les jardins. Nous ne trouvons aussi aucun dessin faisant référence aux folies eugéniques et autres folies « scientifiques » de l'époque (l'élevage ornithologique de Jacob !), aucune représentation « reliant les fantaisies occultistes avec le pressentiment de découvrir la biochimie », aucune production frankensteinienne, aucune « forme en dehors du paradigme des formes existantes », aucun renvoi aux expérimentations démiurgiques du Père[37]. Nous ne rencontrons pas non plus les spécimens « du bestiaire de Drohobycz » (on en a pourtant catalogué près de 120)[38]. La liste des motifs « non exposés » pourrait être encore élargie plus avant[39]. Cette inadéquation ne serait-elle pas tout simplement le résultat du faible niveau artistique des dessins de Schulz ?

36 W. Chmurzyński, „Spotkanie ze *Spotkaniem*" dans *Czytanie Schulza*, op. cit., pp. 273-274.

37 S. Chwin, op. cit., p. 278-285.

38 A. Ossowski, „Drohobyckie bestiarium" dans *Bruno Schulz in memoriam*, op. cit., p. 90.

39 L'analyse de la formation d'images oniriques dans la prose de Schulz livre aussi des

Il n'y a que l'épouse manquée de l'artiste, Józefina Szelińska, a avoir mis, à ce qu'il paraît, plus haut que sa prose ses réussites plastiques. Il est admis aussi que Schulz est en tant qu'écrivain un novateur et en tant que dessinateur un traditionnaliste, assimilant le fond et la forme ce qui est typique à la charnière des deux siècles derniers, alors que la Schulzologie recherche quant à elle plutôt du «nouveau» et nullement l'inscription de cette œuvre dans la tradition[40]. D'où le ton de dédain de quelques-unes des déclarations de chercheurs qui travaillent sur l'œuvre littéraire de Schulz pour ses dessins qui ne seraient «dans une grande mesure que l'accomplissement de rêves (érotiques) cachés»[41]. Par contre pour ce qui est des historiens d'art c'est le ton apologétique qui prévaut. Le plus catégorique est à porter au crédit de l'auteur du catalogue des dessins de Schulz : «autodidacte génial», «plein d'originialité, inimitable», «la grandeur de Schulz est une». Mettre d'un côté Schulz-écrivain et de l'autre Schulz-dessinateur est hors de propos. Egalement hors de propos toute évaluation, même si certains commentaires de l'artiste lui-même pourrait laisser penser le contraire[42].

Le caractère «secondaire» des dessins de Schulz vis-à-vis de sa prose est aussi mis en question du point de vue des changements et bouleversements qui sont apparus dans l'histoire de l'art du XXe siècle, au travers de l'abandon du «paradigme d'avant-garde» qui fut longtemps chez elle dominant. «L'art de Bruno Schulz est l'exemple que ce qui était anachronique hier est aujourd'hui d'avant-garde»[43]. De ce point de vue, l'amateurisme, le manque de métier, le manque de «style» se trouvent être une qualité, qualité qui empêche de tomber dans la facilité de l'érotisme kitsch.

Les controverses et polémiques en ce qui concerne l'évaluation de l'œuvre plastique de Schulz apparaissent donc vides de sens. Ce qui par contre peut à partir de cette évaluation faire surgir des problèmes intéressants c'est l'analyse des possibilités de « faire parler » l'image d'un côté, et d'«imager» le mot d'un autre côté. Il faut avant tout rappeler que dans l'histoire de l'art priment

---

arguments au profit de son 'intransposabilité' dans le langage visuel, cf. J. Jarzębski, „Wstęp" dans *Bruno Schulz. Opowiadania, wybór esejów i listów,* Zakład Naukowy im. Ossolińskich, Wrocław, 1989, en particulier la partie „Obrazowanie".

40 W. Bolecki, op. cit., p. 138.

41 J. Jarzębski, *Brunona Schulza malowanie słowem* dans *Bruno Schulz in memoriam,* op. cit., p. 43.

42 W. Chmurzyński, *Schulziana...,* op. cit., p. 12.

43 E. Kuryluk, op. cit., p. 233.

actuellement les méthodes de recherches sur les relations entre mot/image, en appuyant la réflexion sur l'historicité de notre vision aussi bien que de notre entendement. La pratique de la reconstruction des relations entre les images et leurs sources littéraires – base de la tradition de l'histoire de l'art – est inéluctablement marquée par la perspective de l'interprétation contemporaine, ce qui laisse un large champ pour les associations et interprétations du commentateur[44]. Depuis peu on a aussi mis en avant le postulat de la mise à l'écart du paradigme, jusqu'alors pris en compte, des recherches intégrées qui se traduisent dans la pratique par l'éclairage du monde plastique au moyen de la prose et par le questionnement du langage visuel de Schulz[45]. Jusqu'à ce jour cependant l'on a examiné uniquement son langage poétique. L'analyse de ce langage montre le caractère totalement distinctif de ces deux média : littéraire et plastique, et contredit l'idée de *correspondance.* Le côté peu commun de découverte, d'invention dans la morphologie linguistique de Schulz, le style de l'écrivain, comparable à aucun autre et pour tout dire qui n'appartient qu'à lui, fait face à un répertoire limité et conventionnel de formes plastiques et de moyens traditionnels de mise en image. Apparaît donc la question, jusqu'à quel niveau 'la *mythification* de la réalité' a pu se réaliser dans l'œuvre plastique et si elle était au fond possible ? Il ne s'agit pas ici de la différence de valeur entre les dessins de Schulz et ses romans. Les descriptions scripturaires de Schulz ne peuvent être « illustrées », visualisées, lorsque leur fonction primordiale (...) se trouve être d'ajouter aux choses des propriétés qui ne sont nullement contenues dans leur facticité même. « La chose même », dont Schulz a parlé dans son manifeste, se trouve justement en dehors de la dite chose – elle est toujours une valeur ajoutée[46]. « Il n'est pas possible pour le lecteur de reconstruire par le moyen oculaire l'image [de Schulz], ce qui signifie qu'elle n'est pas ce que l'auteur avait imaginé et ce qu'il a codifié dans la langue littéraire »[47]. Les images poétiques de Schulz ne peuvent être concrétisées, ne peuvent être « vues », même par les yeux de l'imagination. Elles sont comme un magma en perpétuel effervescence, tremblant d'une dynamique intérieure de métaphores à niveaux multiples.

---

44 M. Bal, *Reading 'Rembrandt': beyond the word-image opposition: the Northrop Frye lectures in literary theory,* Cambridge University Press, Cambridge, New York, 1991.

45 M. Szeląg, '„Kataryniarz" Brunona Schulza' dans *W ułamkach zwierciadła,* op. cit.

46 W. Bolecki, *Język poetycki i proza : twórczośc Brunona Schulza,* Zakład Naukowy im. Ossolińskich, Wrocław 1982, p. 228.

47 J. Jarzębski, *Brunona Schulza malowanie słowem,* op. cit., p. 56.

Afin de conclure nous citerons Schulz lui-même : « Et quand je prenais la couleur bleue, par toutes les rues et sur toutes les fenêtres passait le reflet pervenche du printemps, les vitres s'ouvraient une à une en tintant, brillantes, remplies d'azur et de feu du ciel, les rideaux se dressaient sonnant l'alerte et un courant joyeux traversait les mousselines et les oléandres sur les balcons vides, comme si au loin, à l'autre bout de cette très longue allée claire, quelqu'un était apparu et approchait radieux, précédé par la nouvelle, par le pressentiment et des signaux lumineux jetés de borne à borne »[48]. C'est le célèbre fragment de *l'Epoque de génie* qui « commence par le dessin et se termine par la vision de l'arrivée du Messie »[49].

Ce genre d'image, stimulée par le génie de l'écrivain, seul le mot immatériel et insaisissable peut se mesurer à elle et se hisser à sa hauteur.

Traduction de Gilles Renard

[48] Trad. T. Douchy.

[49] W. Panas, *Mesjasz rośnie pomału...*, op. cit., p. 118.

1. **Autoportrait en blouse bleu**
Crayon sur papier, vers 1933
Muzeum Literatury im. A. Mickiewicza, Warszawa

2. Rencontre : un garçon juif et deux jeunes filles dans une ruelle
L'huile sur carton, 1920
Muzeum Literatury im. A. Mickiewicza, Warszawa

3. Introduction
Cliché-verre, 1920-1922
Planche de série *Le Livre idolâtre*
Muzeum Literatury im. A. Mickiewicza, Warszawa

4. Le cirque (Mademoiselle circé et sa troupe)
Cliché-verre, 1920-1922
Planche de série *Le Livre idolâtre*
Muzeum Literatury im. A. Mickiewicza, Warszawa

5. Undula idéal éternel

Cliché-verre, 1920-1922
Planche de série *Le Livre idolâtre*
Muzeum Literatury im. A. Mickiewicza, Warszawa

6. Eunuques et étalons
Cliché-verre, 1920-1922
Planche de série *Le Livre idolâtre*
Muzeum Literatury im. A. Mickiewicza, Warszawa

7. L’Infante et ses nains

Cliché-verre, 1920-1922

Planche de série *Le Livre idolâtre*

Muzeum Literatury im. A. Mickiewicza, Warszawa

8. Trois hommes nus agenouillés devant une femme avec une cravache
Aquarelle, gouache et crayon sur papier, 1920
Muzeum Literatury im. A. Mickiewicza, Warszawa

9. Le retraité et les garçons

Encre de Chine sur papier calque, 1937

Illustration pour le récit « Le Retraité » du volume *Le sanatorium au croque-mort*

Muzeum Literatury im. A. Mickiewicza, Warszawa

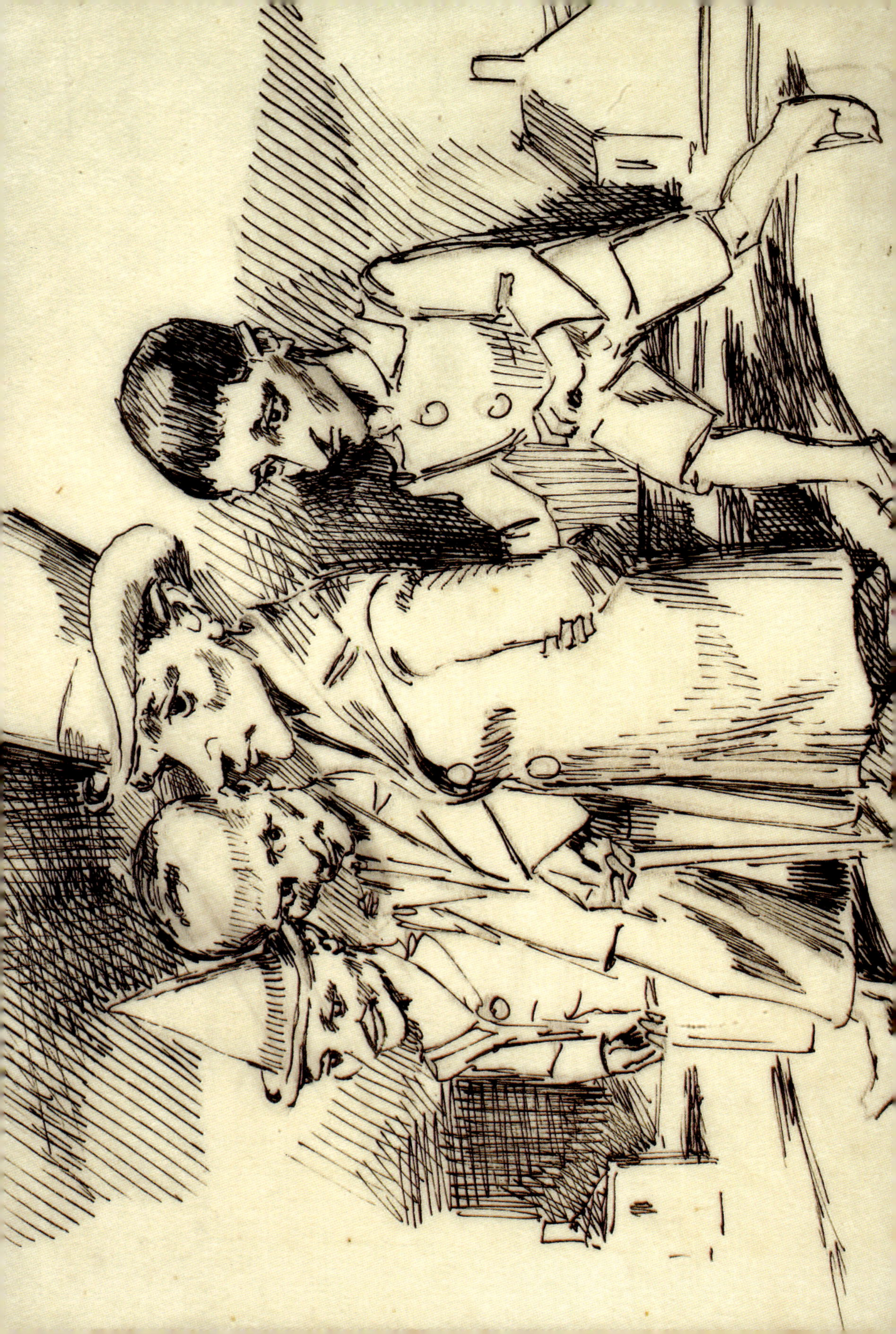

10. Les hassidim au puits

Encre de Chine sur papier calque, vers 1934
Illustration pour un roman perdu *Le Messie* (?)
Muzeum Literatury im. A. Mickiewicza, Warszawa

11. Trois femmes sur une canapé et un «homme-chien» rampant a ses pieds
Crayon sur papier, avant 1933
Muzeum Literatury im. A. Mickiewicza, Warszawa

Schulz au cinéma. Les miniatures des Frères Quay

Johanne Villeneuve – Université du Québec à Montréal

Resumé

*En 1986, les frères Quay proposent, sous la forme d'un court métrage, une adaptation cinématographique de la célèbre nouvelle de Bruno Schulz intitulée « La rue des crocodiles ». Il s'agit d'un film d'animation entièrement tourné en studio, comme le sont la plupart des films des Brothers Quay, où évoluent des figurines, marionnettes en train d'être confectionnées par leurs congénères, poupées, anatomistes et démiurges de pacotille confinés à quelque cabinet ou chambre obscure. Réduisant le quartier tout entier dont parle Schulz dans sa nouvelle à l'espace clos d'un studio, les cinéastes adaptent plutôt librement le texte en fonction d'un univers qui leur est propre. Cependant, il ressort du film une relecture complexe de l'œuvre entière de Schulz, voire une forme de « parenté » poétique qui renvoie les deux œuvres l'une à l'autre. Il apparaît alors que le cinéma d'animation, tel qu'exploré par les Brothers Quay, se trouve déjà en germe dans l'univers poétique Schulzien, de même que dans ses dessins. On y retrouve, plus particulièrement, l'expression d'une densification de la réalité matérielle (celle, peut-être, d'un cabinet de curiosité où se défile autant qu'elle se déploie une mémoire intime), une mise en scène particulière du regard soucieuse du « monde des choses », une iconographie miniaturiste basée sur la répétition, tous ces traits convergeant vers les figures de l'inachèvement et de l'inassouvissement. Cette communication fera donc état de cette parenté et, plus particulièrement, de ce que Schulz apporte, sans le savoir, au cinéma d'animation de la fin du XX*e *siècle.*

En 1986, les frères Quay proposent, sous la forme d'un court métrage, ce qui semble être une adaptation cinématographique du texte de Bruno Schulz intitulé *La rue des crocodiles*, texte tiré des *Boutiques de cannelle*[1]. Il s'agit d'un film d'animation entièrement tourné en studio, comme le sont la plupart des films des Frères Quay, où évoluent des figurines, marionnettes confectionnées ou démontées par leurs congénères, poupées, anatomistes et démiurges de pacotille confinés à quelque cabinet ou chambre obscure. Réduisant le quartier tout entier dont parle Schulz à l'espace clos d'un studio, les cinéastes adaptent librement le texte. Cependant, il ressort du film une relecture de l'œuvre de

[1] Rappelons également le film de Wojciech Has, *Sanatorium pod klepsydrą* (Pologne, 1973).

Schulz, une forme de 'parenté' esthétique qui renvoie les deux œuvres l'une à l'autre. Ainsi, le film emprunte à d'autres textes de Schulz, en particulier à ce discours du père dans le *Traité des mannequins ou la seconde genèse.* De cette relecture émerge, en retour, le sentiment qu'il y a déjà, chez Schulz, quelque chose comme une acuité cinématographique, une sensibilité au monde des « choses » comme aux apparences fluctuantes, aux métamorphoses et à « l'esprit de la matière », à sa présence paradoxalement fantomatique, aux ombres projetées depuis la place de l'halluciné ou du rêveur.

Ce sont ces deux aspects qui constitueront l'approche de Schulz préconisée dans ce texte : une lecture de l'œuvre par le biais du cinéma et une approche du cinéma par le bais d'une œuvre littéraire.

Cinéphilie

Que Schulz aimât le cinéma et que cet amour soit devenu un élément fondamental de son univers, Henri Lewi le souligne déjà dans son ouvrage consacré à l'écrivain[2]. On sait par ailleurs que le frère de Schulz projetait des films dans son cinéma de Drohobycz ; il n'est donc pas exclu de penser que le cinématographe avait une place dans la maison familiale elle-même : séances de projections maisons, réunions familiales devant un écran improvisé. Sur le plan de l'univers poétique de Schulz, le cinéma semble participer de la réminiscence. D'une part, certaines scènes se déroulant au magasin paternel paraissent projetées à la manière d'un film sur des draperies tendues dans le clair-obscur (on pense à « La Nuit de la grande saison » et au texte « La morte saison »)[3] ; d'autre part, comme y insiste Lewi, les images cinématographiques contaminent l'œuvre à travers les jeux d'une esthétique expressionniste[4] dont Schulz avait la passion en tant que cinéphile. La fluidité des images[5], inhérente à l'engrenage même du cinématographe, traverserait aussi l'écriture de Schulz. Mais surtout, dans La nuit de juillet, le narrateur raconte ses soirées estivales au cinéma de Drohobycz, insistant sur l'étrange passage de la salle de cinéma au hall, quand le spectateur éprouve, à travers la difficulté du désillement, le sentiment d'un brouillage entre la projection cinématographique et le monde extérieur. Lewi écrit :

---

2 H. Lewi, *Bruno Schulz ou les stratégies messianiques*, La Table Ronde, Paris, 1989, p. 160.

3 Le premier des deux 'contes' termine *Les boutiques de cannelle,* le second fait partie du *Sanatorium au croque-mort.*

4 H. Lewi, op. cit., p. 161.

5 ibid., p. 160.

Johanne Villeneuve – Université du Québec à Montréal

> Personne n'a mieux évoqué que Schulz le sentiment d'étrangeté qui saisit le cinéphile quand il passe de la salle au hall, cette impression d'être hors du temps puisque sorti du spectacle, et comment l'illusoire du film contamine le réel, faisant apparaître douteuse la présence de la guichetière ou du pompier de service, les réduisant à un statut d'image[6].

Or, cette « impression d'être hors du temps » que fournit l'expérience du spectateur au cinéma, si justement décrite par Schulz, ne révèle-t-elle pas, de manière emblématique, le sentiment plus général d'une époque sans repères, où, pour le dire comme le narrateur des *Boutiques de cannelle,* circule une foule « dépourvue de visages et de caractéristiques »[7] ? — époque du bouleversement économique à Drohobycz, mais aussi celle de la suspension du temps historique entre les deux guerres de masse, suspension liée à l'écroulement d'un empire et à l'incertitude quant à l'avenir, voire au brouillage des anciennes frontières, à la facticité. À rebours, à notre époque, on ne peut manquer d'apercevoir dans l'oeuvre un double effet : l'effacement d'un monde, broyé par la première guerre, et sa persistance à travers les décombres et les témoignages des survivants de la seconde. En tant que lecteurs actuels, pouvons-nous échapper à une telle lecture anachronique ?

Et comment ne pas voir dans les péripéties d'une œuvre partiellement sauvée de l'oubli et brutalement interrompue dans le cours destructeur des disparitions de masse un gage testamentaire ? L'expérience de l'écriture littéraire ne commence-t-elle pas, chez Schulz, par le geste de la transmission épistolaire, sorte de « legs » prémonitoire et tragiquement ironique (puisque la grande part de la correspondance de l'auteur aura été détruite)[8] ? C'est donc qu'il doit y avoir une « destination intime » constitutive de l'écriture, valeur testamentaire inscrite dans le déroulement même du souvenir d'enfance et de sa narration. La littérature tient alors à la nécessité d'une relation épistolaire ; mais elle éclôt à la surface d'une époque surréelle, à la faveur de liens, de fils tendus au-dessus des abîmes. L'importance de cette impression se confirme à travers l'expérience que Schulz fait au cinéma, soit celle d'une

[6] ibid., p. 161. (C'est moi qui souligne)

[7] B.Schulz, « La nuit de la grande saison » dans *Les boutiques de cannelle, Œuvres,* Denoël, Paris, 2004 p. 117.

[8] Voir à ce sujet la préface de Jerzy Ficowski dans B. Schulz, *Correspondance, Œuvres,* op. cit., p.526–539. Texte publié également dans B. Schulz, *Correspondance et essais critiques,* Denoël, Paris, 1991, p.17–33.

zone incertaine, aux frontières indécidables, à la temporalité trouble, entre le sommeil et la veille. La « rue des crocodiles » est une véritable figure, une mise en abyme de cette zone dont l'œuvre entière de Schulz se nourrit : sur la carte de la ville,

> les environs de la rue des Crocodiles faisaient une tache blanche comparable à celle qui, dans les géographies, signale les régions polaires, les pays incertains ou inexplorés[9].

La « tache blanche » est aussi ce qui inonde la rétine de l'œil quand celui-ci advient brusquement à la lumière. Elle traduit parfaitement l'impression subie au passage de la salle obscure du cinéma à la lumière du hall.

Projection/animation

Mais surtout, l'obsession que Schulz entretint à l'égard de sa propre mythographie littéraire, il a pu en reconnaître le prolongement dans le cinéma, à la faveur d'un caractère de nouveauté, d'une dimension utopique encore inégalée, comme si le cinématographe combinait de manière exemplaire et parfaitement lisse les aspirations demeurées contrariées chez Schulz lui-même par la linéarité de l'écriture : un réalisme du détail doublé d'une force de fabulation, une exaltation du fétiche et de la trace en même temps qu'un effet de fictionnalisation produit par la projection surdimensionnée d'un espace : celui des images à l'écran. La technique de « projection » est elle-même constitutive de la poétique de Schulz, à la différence près que la surface de projection est, chez lui, tantôt celle de la carte (cartes et plans de la ville ou d'un quartier, mais aussi « planches »), tantôt celle du livre : ainsi commence, par exemple, les boutiques de cannelle :

> Au mois de juillet, mon père partait aux eaux et nous laissait, ma mère, mon frère aîné et moi, en pâture aux journées d'été, blanches de feu et enivrantes. Nous feuilletions, étourdis de lumière, le grand livre des vacances, dont chaque page scintillait de soleil et conservait tout en son fond, sucrée jusqu'à la pâmoison, la pulpe des poires dorées[10].

---

[9] B. Schulz, *Œuvres,* op. cit., p. 87.

[10] ibid., p. 19.

La poésie se déploie à la manière de retables soudainement animés par la lumière, ou de ces cartes dépliées, offrant la projection animée de l'enfance, tantôt lumineuse, tantôt sombre, fabulations délivrées par le geste démiurgique du père. Dans ses *Déclarations sur des projets et créations littéraires,* Schulz écrit :

> Le germe initial de mes 'Oiseaux' fut par exemple un scintillement de papiers peints dans un champ de vision sombre – rien de plus. [...] Le germe initial de 'Printemps' fut l'image d'un album de timbre-poste, qui rayonnait au centre de la vision, brillant d'une puissance allusive extraordinaire, une charge si agressive qu'on ne pouvait passer outre[11].

Les figures de ces livres, cartes, albums de timbres, tapisseries s'animent littéralement chez Schulz, conférant à toute image les qualités cinétiques et métamorphiques de l'écran de cinéma. Les images littéraires de Schulz (ces fameuses métaphores), sont souvent le produit d'une animation par la lumière, précisément à la façon du cinématographe en tant qu'appareil d'enregistrement et de projection des empreintes lumineuses. La projection devient alors le mode de prédilection d'une energeia poétique. Partant très souvent d'un objet discret, d'une localité restreinte, d'une fragilité quelconque, Schulz projette un monde, déplie les feuillets racornis d'un souvenir, les ouvre sur la dimension cosmogonique et le devenir collectif. La nouvelle *La rue des crocodiles* émerge d'un tiroir :

> Mon père conservait dans le tiroir inférieur de son vaste bureau un beau plan ancien de notre ville. C'était tout un volume de parchemins in-folio qui, réunis par des rubans de toile, formaient une immense carte murale représentant un panorama à vol d'oiseau[12].

Au début du *Sanatorium au croque-mort,* le narrateur décrit avec exubérance son rapport idyllique au Livre, insistant encore sur sa dimension projective et utopique :

---

11 ibid., p. 512.

12 ibid., p. 86.

> Parfois mon père se détachait du Livre et s'éloignait. Je restais seul, alors le vent traversait les pages et les images se levaient. [...] À cette époque, ma mère n'était pas encore là. Je passais mes journées seul avec mon père, dans notre chambre grande comme le monde[13].

Que les pages et les images d'un livre puissent se « lever », grandir dans l'espace d'une chambre, se dresser à la manière des apparitions, cela tient bien, à l'époque où Schulz écrit, de l'art cinématographique. En revanche, ses personnages rapetissent, en l'occurrence le père qui n'a de cesse, dans *Les Boutiques de cannelle,* de s'enfoncer entre les lattes du plancher, de se mélanger à la poussière, d'atteindre le miniature, jusqu'à la disparition. Dans *Le Sanatorium au croque-mort,* il devient une mouche virevoltant dans le magasin familial.

C'est que le regard projectif, qui permet de voir dans l'exiguïté de la chambre ou les limites de la page l'étendue cosmique, fait de tout être sa chose, sa miniature. Or l'intérêt porté à ces miniatures en révèle l'affinité secrète avec le cosmos, le Très Haut. Les détails de l'enfance, les restes diurnes, les pigments enfouis de la matière accèdent aux dimensions cosmogoniques. Si le très grand se voit miniaturisé, le rebut, le débris, est à rebours exalté chez Schulz sous l'effet d'un gros plan. Le narrateur du *Sanatorium* raconte :

> Nous allons donc recueillir allusions, gros plans terrestres, arrêts et étapes sur les chemins de notre vie, débris d'un miroir cassé. Nous allons ramasser par petits morceaux ce qui est un et indivisible — notre grande époque, l'époque de génie de notre vie[14].

Cette « grande époque » est bien celle, littéralement, de la « camera » - cabinet de curiosité, *camera obscura* de l'enfance, nouvellement animée, chambre où le monde découvre à la faveur du clair-obscur ses proportions infinies, non pas cette fois à la manière intime d'un Marcel Proust, mais à travers le déliement solennel du mythe de la création. La modestie du créateur y rencontre la mythomanie du rêveur.

Autre chose encore motive le rapport entre Schulz et le cinéma. Dans la mesure où celui-ci présente un monde de spectres sous l'apparence toujours

[13] ibid., p. 126.

[14] ibid., p. 138.

délivrée du vivant, Schulz pouvait très certainement y faire l'expérience contradictoire d'une distanciation auratique et d'une proximité, d'un désir haptique, celui d'approcher, de toucher le vivant par le truchement des images en mouvement, de leurs engrenages, de leur fabrique étrangement sensuelle. Pourraient en témoigner le discours du père dans le « Traité des mannequins »:

> ...la mort n'est qu'une apparence sous laquelle se cachent des formes de vie inconnues. Leur échelle est infinie, leurs nuances sont inépuisables. Par de multiples et précieux arcanes le Démiurge a créé de nombreuses espèces douées du pouvoir de se reproduire[15].

Cette faculté, qu'a justement le cinématographe, de lier reproduction, spectralité et formes de vie, est au centre de l'attention des penseurs du cinéma au cours de son émergence en tant que dispositif artistique, au moment où Schulz écrit et fréquente le cinéma : Walter Benjamin, Vsevolod Poudovkine, Siegfried Kracauer et André Bazin l'auront conçu dans ces termes : art fondé sur la reproductibilité pour Benjamin, faisant apparaître l'aura pour une dernière fois, à l'instar de la photographie dont il est issu[16]; transformation du matériau « mort » de l'image photographique en « une forme cinématique vivante » pour Poudovkine[17]; « rédemption de la réalité physique » pour Kracauer[18]; et pour Bazin, cet « arrachement de l'être au fleuve de la durée », prolongement technique et logique du « complexe de la momie » inauguré par l'art de l'embaumement à l'origine des arts plastiques[19]. Au début du recueil *Les boutiques de cannelles,* le narrateur a l'impression de voir, dans un oiseau endormi,

---

15 ibid., p. 51.

16 W. Benjamin, *L'œuvre d'art à l'époque de sa reproduction mécanisée, dans Gesammelte Schriften, vol. 1, tome 2,* R. Tiedemann et H. Schweppenhaüser dir., Suhrkamp Verlag, Francfort, 1978, p. 709–739.

17 V. Poudovkine, *Le fondement de l'art cinégraphique* (tiré de *Cinéa Ciné pour tous et Film Technique,* 1924 et 1939), dans *L'art du cinéma,* Seghers, Paris, 1960, p. 189.

18 S. Kracauer, *Theory of Film. The Redemption of Physical Reality,* Oxford Univesity Press, Oxford, (1960) 1974. Kracauer a commencé à élaborer cette idée depuis son étude de la photographie en 1927.

19 A. Bazin, *Ontologie de l'image photographique,* dans *Qu'est-ce que le cinéma ?,* Les Éditions du Cerf, Paris, 1997, p. 9.

> la momie de [son] père, réduite par dessiccation[20].

Dans le *Sanatorium,* Joseph décrit le matin printanier:

> Il naît soudain une atmosphère matinale, atmosphère d'avant le temps, dans ces longues allées vides où les morts reposés se réveillent un rang après l'autre à une aube toute neuve[21].

On trouve, chez Schulz une sorte de révélation cinématographique qui passe par une description précise, et pourtant parfaitement onirique, de la Galicie « comme pays fantôme » - pour reprendre l'éloquente expression de Laurence Sigal-Klagsbald[22] —, mais aussi par le souvenir d'enfance comme empreinte photographique à laquelle l'écriture rend une âme, cette anima dont le cinématographe semble être l'expression matérielle la plus parfaite. Sur le modèle médiumnique du cinéma, l'écriture de Schulz tend à soustraire le temps à sa propre corruption[23] (Bazin écrivait, à propos de la photographie constitutive de l'ontologie du cinéma, qu'elle « embaumait » le temps en le « soustrayant seulement à sa propre corruption ») en même temps qu'elle en anime la corruption sous la forme de restes diurnes, de souvenirs fragmentaires, d'archives personnelles livrées à l'oubli, quant ce n'est au grand déni familial.

Les Frères Quay

Si Schulz n'est jamais vraiment sorti de sa petite ville d'enfance, les jumeaux Stephen et Timothy Quay se sont exilés de leur Pennesylvanie natal pour fonder, à Londres, un studio qui leur permet de renouer avec un cinéma artisanal, plus près du cabinet de Svankmajer, cinéaste d'animation tchèque, que d'Hollywood. Leur cinéma est consacré littéralement à l'animation d'une mémoire fabriquée, œuvre de collectionneurs ou de surréalistes déconstructionnistes et anachroniques, empruntant davantage aux cultures d'Europe Centrale qu'à l'iconographie nord-américaine. Leurs films, bien que réalisés à notre époque et bénéficiant de la technologie actuelle, ont une double patine : sur le plan thématique, leur univers est celui des choses anciennes, oubliées,

20 B. Schulz, *Œuvres,* op. cit., p. 40.

21 ibid., p. 173.

22 L. Sigal-Klagsbald, *Avant propos au catalogue La république des rêves,* Musée d'art et d'histoire du Judaïsme, Denoël, Paris, 2004, p. 16.

23 A. Bazin, op. cit., p. 14.

déchues ; sur le plan esthétique, leurs films ont l'air d'appartenir à une époque lointaine, époque fascinée autant par les machines modernes que par la survivance de l'ancien. On les dirait issus d'un dialogue sans transition avec Walter Benjamin ou Valéry, qui écrivait :

> L'homme n'est l'homme qu'à sa surface. Lève la peau, dissèque : ici commencent les machines. Puis tu te perds dans une substance inexplicable, étrangère à tout ce que tu sais et qui est pourtant l'essentielle[24].

À une différence près, cependant, puisque au cœur de la mécanique elle-même se révèle la fantastique altérité de l'organique. Les films des Frères Quay semblent surgir des ruines de ce monde industriel auquel fait si souvent allusion Schulz, pour connecter les vestiges des rêves du XIXe siècle aux déshérences technologiques de la fin du XXe, traçant l'ellipse, la courbe « *archangélique* », eux aussi, au-dessus des abîmes historiques.

Leur atelier permet l'élaboration d'un véritable « cinéma de chambre » - films à haute teneur onirique, ramenant les deux frères à la fantasmagorie de l'enfance, mais surtout, à l'enfermement volontaire dans ce que Schulz appelait lui-même, à propos de sa ville, un « microcosme indépendant » situé « au bord de l'éternité »[25]. C'est sur ce plan que leur univers croise celui de Bruno Schulz de la manière la plus évidente : l'expression maniaque d'une mythologie enfantine, où les objets quotidiens, les choses, les détails occupent une place démesurée, font « gros plan », sous la condition d'une temporalité étrange[26] et d'un élan démiurgique : regard et temporalité de l'enfance, de la petite ville ou du petit studio, de la chambre du dormeur — espaces de proliférations des détails, de grossissement du petit et de miniaturisation du monde ; espaces de mémoires comme de banissements où les choses quotidiennes perdent leurs contours et gagnent en intensité sous l'effet d'une désorientation esthétique.

---

24 P. Valéry, *Cahier B*, 1910, Paris, 1930, p. 39–40, cité par Walter Benjamin, *Paris, Capitale du XIXe siècle,* Cerf, Paris, 1989, p. 422. Dans la version parue en DVD, le commentaire sonore que les Frères Quay consacrent au film fait allusion aux célèbres passages parisiens célébrés par Benjamin dans son livre. Bien que ne mentionnant pas Benjamin, les cinéastes mentionnent qu'ils se sont basés sur ces passages pour élaborer la zone où se déroule *The Street of Crocodile Phantom Museums. The Short Films of the Quay Brothers,* Zeitgeist Video, 2007.

25 B. Schulz, *La république des rêves,* Musée d'art et d'histoire du Judaïsme, Denoël, Paris, 2004, p. 2 : « La ville et la région se sont enfermées dans un microcosme indépendant, elles se sont installées à leurs risques et périls au bord de l'éternité. »

Chez Schulz, la figuration la plus réussie de cette désorientation se trouve dans le parcours que fait l'enfant, un soir, dans sa ville devenue soudainement méconnaissable, alors que

> les rues se multiplient, se brouillent et échangent leurs place dans la pénombre… [alors que s'ouvrent] des rues doubles […], des sosies de rues… […] L'imagination aberrante et enchantée recrée les plans illusoires d'une ville qu'elle croit connaître, plans où ces voies ont leur place et leur nom, cependant que la nuit, dans sa fécondité inépuisable, ne trouve rien d'autre à faire que de continuer à produire d'irréelles configurations[27].

Chez les frères Quay, cet espace n'est plus celui de la ville, mais celui du studio. Amateurs de baroque, ils s'intéressent aux collections : les objets d'art et les instruments scientifiques, mais saisis dans leur état d'abandon, comme après le passage du dernier homme ; les planches d'anatomie, les cartes, les cahiers et les livres empoussiérés, les meubles à tiroirs sont légions ; les marionnettes, les automates et les mannequins peuplent leurs films, tirés chaque fois de ces musées du sommeil dont on évoque la possibilité dans un autre de leurs films *The Comb. From the Museums of Sleep* (1991). Sorte de « république des rêves », leur univers semble tenir dans le creux d'une main, voire entre les doigts d'un diamantaire. Et comme le diamant qui, aussi minuscule soit-il, procure à l'œil qui s'en approche d'incommensurables visions, le territoire des frères Quay invite à de curieux parcours : l'espace clos du studio, celui des plus exigus de la camera obscura, échappe pourtant ; il fuit à travers les multiples passages et tracés du regard, les jeux de focalisation et de défocalisation de l'image, les perspectives tronquées, les découpes de lumière et les ombres, les accélérations

---

26 Les Quay auront mis six mois à tourner leur petit film de 21 minutes. La durée de fabrication de certains plans ou de certaines séquences peut parfois produire une étrangeté sur le plan de l'image finie. Car la pellicule conserve des traces infimes d'altérité, traces étrangement manifestes de cette durée ; celle-ci produit une temporalité toujours tributaire d'une résistance, d'une persistance dans l'image et qui révèle le croisement entre un temps naturel (celui des choses) et un temps mécanique (celui des appareils). C'est sans compter le travail sonore de la musique, de la rythmique des machines, et le rythme même des corps en mouvement que les Quay privilégient en créant de toute pièce une chorégraphie adaptée à la musique de Leszek Jankowski.

27 B. Schulz, *Œuvres,* op. cit., p. 76.

aléatoires du mouvement, les filtres qui travestissent la vision, et ces trajectoires de la caméra qui évoquent davantage une mécanique optique que la vision humaine.

Davantage qu'une simple adaptation d'une nouvelle de Schulz, le film *The Street of Crocodiles,* à partir du motif du « fil » (fil de la marionnette, fil dans l'engrenage d'une machine à tisser, fil de la filiation entre le père et sa créature), récupère plutôt des « morceaux » de l'œuvre littéraire de Schulz pour en jouer une partition inusitée : morceaux d'une œuvre morcelée d'emblée. L'espace quadrillé par le film est celui d'une boutique de tailleur (on pense, bien sûr, au magasin du père dans le texte de Schulz) ; mais le spectateur comprend aussi que cet espace est lui-même emboîté dans celui du cinématographe, celui de la caméra-machine et de sa lentille, celui-là, déjà lui-même emboîté dans un étrange appareil fantasmagorique d'animation et de reproduction que manipule un démiurge au début du film, sur la scène d'un théâtre vide. Ce jeu d'échelle et d'emboîtements confirme la fonction des miniatures chez les frères Quay : c'est dans le détail de la matière en apparence immobile, dans le rapprochement des choses discrètes, que se découvre ce que Schulz désignait comme étant « primordial ». Dans le « primordial » se cacherait, selon lui, une événementialité irrévocable :

> Ici tout se joue une seule fois, irrévocablement[28].

Et pourtant, l'œuvre de Schulz, comme celle des frères Quay, s'appuie davantage sur des procédés de descriptions que sur des procédés narratifs ; la mise en intrigue épouse une temporalité cyclique (qu'on pense aux saisons du *Sanatorium au Croque-mort*). Celle du film des frères Quay repose sur la machination du « carrousel » et la désarticulation d'une valse. Chez Schulz, le mode itératif en impose au point de confondre le lecteur et de le faire glisser, comme nous le disions plus tôt, hors du temps, sur la crête d'une enfance immémoriale. C'est que l'événement, dans un cas comme dans l'autre, ne constitue ni un moment de la narration, ni même le seul foyer du souvenir, mais la convergence des affinités entre la matière et l'idéalité, entre l'expérience et l'image, entre le mutisme de l'enfant et les possibilités du langage. L'irrévocable, c'est ce mouvement, ce processus qui engage l'écriture à recommencer, à traverser la densité de l'expérience et de la matière, à passer tel un spectre d'un plan à un autre, du plan d'ensemble (groupe, paysage, quartier,

[28] B. Schulz, *Œuvres*, op. cit., p. 3.

ville) au gros plan[29] ; du macrocosme au microcosme et vice versa, sans jamais perdre de vue la démultiplication des plans. Schulz, comme Benjamin, est de ceux qui renversent l'allégorie platonicienne de la caverne et donnent à penser que la projection de l'image se fait depuis l'arrière-fond de la matière, que là se trouve le secret de la lumière en tant que révélation - constat tautologique, s'il en est un, mais où prospère une conception nouvelle de l'image.

Le film des frères Quay permet de redécouvrir la force de ce mouvement programmé dans l'écriture. Il y a, chez Schulz, une géométrie que la référence aux seuls procédés surréalistes de « collage » et de « condensation » ne réussit pas à cerner : la traversée des plans, dont le regard chez lui est tributaire, ne consiste pas simplement à exciter les oppositions, à braquer les conditions du réel en les mobilisant vers l'inconscient ; le montage hautement descriptif de Schulz n'opère pas une rencontre entre des images, mais une véritable densification du souvenir en tant qu'image. Le montage, cette traversée des plans, œuvre ici à l'intérieur même d'une image, rendant visible le vaste champ d'empathie qui lie la matière à l'esprit ; d'où cette sensibilité partagée par les frères Quay pour cette géométrie du regard déployée dans le cadre de l'image et non seulement, selon les termes usuels du montage filmique, dans le rapport *entre* les images. La densification de l'image en est le procédé esthétique le plus révélateur : épaisseur du monde des choses, multiplication des filtres, retour obstiné des mêmes motifs, des poses et des attitudes, concaténation des vitesses de déplacement et de déroulement de l'image, viscosité et frémissements de la lumière. La réalité filmique n'en paraît que plus dense, découpée et dégradée. Le cinéma des frères Quay donne à percevoir l'attitude fondamentale de Schulz : celle de l'enfant disséquant le

[29] On notera parallèlement à cet usage du gros plan dans l'écriture de Schulz une constante de son œuvre artistique : ses dessins, proches de l'art de la caricature, reposent très souvent sur un grossissement exagéré de la tête et du visage d'un sujet. Les hommes surtout offrent au regard une tête démesurée par rapport au corps miniaturisé, dont l'expression du visage est si intense et détaillée qu'elle agit exactement comme un gros plan au cinéma. Contrairement à ce qu'un visage produit dans l'art habituel du dessin, la «visagéité» du gros plan cinématographique produit une sorte de rupture avec l'espace. Le gros plan dénature en quelque sorte l'objet et le fait sortir de son milieu. Tels sont les visages et les têtes nombreuses, grossies par l'art de Schulz : des gros plans de visages appliqués de manière inhabituelle et parfois grotesque sur des corps miniatures qui semblent appartenir à un autre espace. L'effet est saisissant, car la dimension expressive du visage, agissant à son tour comme son propre cadre, témoigne de singularités, d'une intériorité et d'un imaginaire, tandis que les corps miniaturisés semblent noyés dans l'espace social de la répétition, plus anonyme et plus réaliste.

cadavre de la Création et trouvant, en place et lieu de la mort, une « autre vie »: la pulsation de la fable.

Dans le film *The Street of Crocodiles,* la puissance fantasmagorique de Schulz prend une tournure plus sombre et plus grave, littéralement comme au figuré. Les figurines, dont les orbites sont vides et les crânes ouverts, s'animent derrière des écrans flous, encrassés, qui perturbent l'accès à la connaissance : accès bloqué au père ? au monde secret de l'érotisme et de la reproduction ? Plus loin, elles défont une marionnette qu'elles reconfectionnnent à la manière d'un rituel qui aurait perdu son sens. Mais surtout, des organes sexuels tronqués, des semblants d'organes, comme si ils avaient été réaménagés par un anatomiste amateur, attirent les figurines aux prises avec un désir inassouvi de créer : la matérialité de ce qui aspire à la vie et à la sensualité, de ce qui cherche désespérément à transfigurer l'automate, la machine. Ce que Schulz décrit dans son texte : le caractère imitatif du quartier, l'impossibilité d'y voir se réaliser pleinement quelque chose, l'amorce des gestes toujours suspendus, la fermentation stérile des désirs et leur précocité, tout cela, les frères Quay l'ont pris à la lettre : les figurines entretiennent l'espoir d'une révélation qui n'advient jamais. Les choses se languissent, échouent à se connecter, à travers une véritable chorégraphie mécanique du faire-semblant.

Créations/Cinéma

En relisant Schulz avec le film, on saisit davantage la portée de la figure du « père » comme figure contradictoire, *fantomachique,* à la fois primordiale, créatrice, et velléitaire. Comme si se dressait, en guise de filiation et de transmission entre le père et le fils, l'œuvre de Schulz, sa destination, telle une réappropriation par le langage des secrets de la matière et de son pouvoir de génération, sorte de « lettre au père[30] » transmuée, consécration de l'inachèvement, de l'inassouvissement, mais aussi, paradoxalement, de la maîtrise de l'artiste. En d'autres termes, l'œuvre pose la question du rapport entre le savoir faire de l'artiste, toujours tributaire d'un apprentissage, et le fantasme de la création, avec ses figures idéales, son lot de métaphores qui ont pour creuset le corps morcelé du père et celui, absent, de la mère.

Dans ce contexte, la matérialité de l'écriture, sans relâche sublimée par le jeu des images, apparaît, chez Schulz, fournir la stratégie ultime de l'artiste. Elle permet au dessinateur d'atteindre le degré d'idéalité nécessaire à l'expression du souvenir, d'en saisir le temps sans compromission aucune ; elle

[30] Ceci est, bien sûr, une allusion à Kafka: F. Kafka, *Lettre au père,* Gallimard, Paris, 2002.

permet d'arraisonner le désir, encore si délibérément puérile dans les dessins de Schulz, aux fins d'une projection du monde qui soit à la fois (et ironiquement) secrète et mythographique. C'est ici que s'inscrit le cinéma dans son œuvre, en tant qu'expérience de projection où la réalité matérielle la plus banale s'hyperbolise à travers le mythe, et où l'espace restreint de la chambre (*camera*) s'affirme dans l'espace public.

Image tirée du film "The Street of Crocodiles" de Stephen et Timothy Quay.
Avec l`authorisation de Zeitgeist Films / By courtesy of Zeitgeist Films.

Image tirée du film “The Street of Crocodiles” de Stephen et Timothy Quay.
Avec l`authorisation de Zeitgeist Films / By courtesy of Zeitgeist Films.

Image tirée du film "The Street of Crocodiles" de Stephen et Timothy Quay.
Avec l`authorisation de Zeitgeist Films / By courtesy of Zeitgeist Films.

Reminiscences

Elżbieta Ficowska - Warsaw, Poland

Thank you for inviting me to this session on Bruno Schulz, and special thanks to the organizers of this symposium at McGill, especially Mr. Stanisław Latek. I am here to replace my late husband, Jerzy Ficowski, writer and historian, who devoted himself to making Schulz's life and work better known.

The story starts in 1942, when Jerzy Ficowski was still young, an 18-year old poet. He happened to read *Sklepy Cynamonowe,* and was so enthralled, that he immediately wrote Schulz a letter, expressing his admiration and belief that Schulz was the epoch's greatest writer. Jerzy long waited for a reply. Only in the spring of 1943 did he learn that Schulz had been killed on 19 November 1942... and so had probably never received the letter.

Therefore, unable to channel his admiration directly to Schulz, young Ficowski decided to set it down in writing. His glowing appraisal of *Sklepy Cynamonowe* appeared in essay form, as *Regiony Wielkiej Herezji.* Ficowski himself considered his early work imperfect, but it was the basis for his continued explorations of the enchanted world of Schulz's creativity.

Admiration and enchantment were not enough; Ficowski sought action. He started searching for every trace of Schulz's life and work. A very daunting task at the time, as Schulz's whole world, all he had held near and dear, had been wiped out together with him. So my husband undertook a detective's task. He searched everywhere, in Poland and throughout the world, he talked to people who had known Schulz, Bruno's colleagues and pupils, he collected all Schulz memorabilia, letters, drawings, sketches, photos and documents. These later turned out to be priceless sources for Schulz' biography. Warsaw's Museum of Literature has now purchased a major part of my husband's collections of Schulz artwork, which is therefore available to us all as to the public.

It was my good fortune to spend 40 years at my husband's side, and I therefore witnessed his overwhelming fascination with Schulz. For example, I remember a sweltering summer in town, when we sat by the telephone waiting for *The Messiah.* We had received a letter from New York, from an unknown Alex Schultz who claimed to be the illegitimate son of Bruno's brother, Izydor. Alex told us he had recently had a mysterious call from the Ukraine, from a person offering to sell him the manuscript of *The Messiah* for $ 30,000. However, Alex first wanted an appraisal from my husband, the only person who could authenticate the manuscript reliably. My husband was stunned, for he himself had been fruitlessly searching for the original manuscript. He invited Alex over.

When Alex came to meet us in Warsaw, we were thunderstruck. He was the image of Bruno Schulz. So his story was perhaps true, though his siblings in New York thought it was invented. At any rate, Alex had asked the Ukrainian to meet him together with my husband in Warsaw, to receive payment after an appraisal of the manuscript. So my husband spent our holidays by the phone, listening for the door-bell... but no one came. Yet we had felt *The Messiah* was so close at hand...

On another day, we had a visit from the Ambassador of Sweden. In a half whisper, he told us that some Ukrainian diplomat, during a reception at the Hungarian Embassy, had surreptitiously revealed knowledge of the whereabouts of *The Messiah*. Together, Alex and the Swedish Ambassador started planning a trip to Ukraine. My husband was of course also eager to go. But the Ambassador fell ill and after his death no one could retrace the mysterious informant.

May I add that what is today happening in Drohobycz is very important for further knowledge and research on Bruno Schulz. Dr. Wiera Meniok told us yesterday about the invaluable work she and her University are doing to preserve Schulz' memory. I had the privilege to attend the Schulz Festival she and her students organized last November. It was an amazing experience. I strongly encourage you to take part in any such future event.

Dr. Meniok devised a fantastic closing ceremony for the Festival. We all gathered at the site of Schulz's tragic assassination, where a memorial plaque had been installed. There was a reading of passages from Schulz's work; it was a moving, memorable moment. Then we proceeded in the dark, torches alight in our hands, to several other sites important for Schulz. Again, there were readings from his literary work, by a different person in each place. Schulz's writing was cited in Polish for the most part, for it is best grasped in the original and is singularly difficult to translate. Ukrainian was also used of course. But I'm impressed that Dr. Meniok herself learned Polish, eager to appreciate the nuances and wealth of Schulz's own thought and language.

This unforgettable pilgrimage, all across the landmarks Bruno Schulz had held dearest, was the most fitting tribute I have seen to his memory.

Translated from Polish by Teresa Romer

Mój nieocalony

Tyle już lat
na mojej antresoli z belek
między sufitem a sienią
ćmi światłość wiekuista na 25 wat
zaciemniona pstrzynami much
za barykadą makulatury
On tam jest nakręca zegarek
nie wygania pająków śpi

Chyba już przetłumaczył wszystkie sęki
Jego cień nieruchomy tynkiem zarasta
czasami nie ma go nawet
po godzinie policyjnej
bawi w Hajdarabadzie
odmyka kolejne słoje
wchodzi w drewno coraz drzewiej i drzewiej

W nie malowaną deskę
sen mój dzisiaj zapukał do niego
Panie Brunonie już można
niech pan schodzi

A on czeka na niedoczekanie
nie może słyszeć mojego snu
on nikt
trzeźwiejszy niż ktokolwiek
wie że
nie ma antresoli
ani światłości
ani mnie

Jerzy Ficowski

Mon non-sauvé

À la mémoire de Bruno Schulz

Depuis tant d'années
au-dessus des poutres de ma mezzanine
entre le plafond et le vestibule
luit une lumière éternelle de 25 watts
obscurcie par les crottes des mouches
derrière une barricade de vieux imprimés
Il est là-haut il remonte sa montre
il ne chasse pas les araignées il dort

Il a traduit déjà tous les nœuds du bois
le crépi couvre peu à peu son ombre immobile
il s'absente parfois même
après l'heure du couvre-feu
il se promène à Haïderabad
il entrouvre une à une les veines du bois
il s'enfonce dans le bois de plus en plus bois de plus
en plus ancien

Mon rêve aujourd'hui a frappé chez lui
Toc toc toc contre le bois brut
Cher Bruno ça y est on peut
descendez donc

Et lui cependant il attend l'inespérable
il ne peut entendre mon rêve
lui qui n'est personne
plus lucide qu'aucun autre
il le sait il n'y a ni mezzanine
ni lumière
ni moi

Jerzy Ficowski
(Traduction de Jacques Burko)

Druk i oprawa:
Poligrafia Inspektoratu Towarzystwa Salezjańskiego
ul. Konfederacka 6, 30-306 Kraków, tel. (012) 266 40 00